CRAFT BEER MARKl
BRACE FOR

By Mark Colburn

Shinerunner Publishing, Walnut Creek, California, USA Copyright Pending 2015

ISBN 9780692503911

Praise for *Craft Beer Marketing & Distribution*

Mark and has spent many years in the Bay Area marketing and distributing some of America's leading craft beers. He is passionate and thoughtful about craft beer.

Jim Koch – Chairman, Boston Beer Company

Mark Colburn has developed into an inquisitive thinker and marketer of beer. He is continually searching for creative ways and distinctive methods to develop beer brands. He has become a student of the beer industry over the past decade and constantly uses his marketing background and focus to trumpet the KDA's of beer brands. Check out his new book to expand your knowledge of the beer industry and learn new ways to see how brands are built!

Bob Stahl – Former President of DBI Beverage and
Golden Brands Distributing

With the craft beer market experiencing phenomenal growth, Mark Colburn has been integral in educating Walgreens team members about the many details of this category. His efforts have allowed us to make more informed decisions in respect to the merchandising and promotion of craft beers. With Mark's help, Walgreens store managers can make better decisions on which brands to promote. Mark has discussed the direction of the craft beer market, and helped position Walgreens to capitalize on emerging trends.

Gorman Moy – Walgreens Senior Manager –
Retail and Pharmacy

I have worked with Mark for ten years and have not met anyone that has the creative marketing energy and passion that he has. I have no clue how he comes up with his ideas but they have certainly helped Mendocino Brewing. In this book you'll learn about beverage marketing and distribution. The real life case histories that Mark shares will provide you with ideas and methods to succeed in today's tough beverage environment. I strongly recommend this book for any beverage professional.

Joseph Frankel – Regional Sales Manager,
Mendocino Brewing Company

As Britain's Director-General of Trade and Investment in the United States for four and a half years, I have seen the work of Mark Colburn at both first and second hand. Mark's efforts at helping UK companies in the food and beverage industry have been outstanding. He has brought to his work unbounded enthusiasm, complete dedication and in-depth knowledge, which he continues to replenish, of the United States food and beverage industry, at all levels.

Sir Alistair Hunter, KCMG – former Director of
Trade and Investment – The Americas

"Your (Mark Colburn's) passion and advocacy, not just for the Guayaki Brand, but for all brands that you represent, is something I have not seen paralleled as I have gone around the country working with industry DSD partners, seriously!"

Mateo Sluder – Regional Sales Manager,
Guayaki -Yerba Mate

Introduction

Mark Colburn, an East Bay native born in Oakland, California earned a Bachelor of Science in Business Administration, concentration Marketing and a Master of Science in Marketing with a concentration in Advertising and thesis on product cannibalism in the beverage industry. As a youngster he preferred to "channel surf" ads instead of watching regular programming. He still thinks there is hope for a 24 hour all advertising cable station (!). After graduate school, Mark went into the advertising agency business as a research analyst. Working for Grey Advertising, he was on the team that launched Kikkoman Light and enjoyed working with the creative teams on strategy and new business presentations. He got his first "taste" of the beverage category when Grey pitched for the then-popular, California Cooler account. For his efforts on California Cooler he was tasked to help prepare the presentation on Shasta soft drinks where he built a market share representation of Coke, Pepsi, and other competitors out of assorted soft drink packages. This combination of bottles, six packs, PET Liter bottles and others graphically depicted the uphill battle that Shasta faced then – all on the executive conference room table.

After Grey, Mark went on to win the American Association of Advertising Agencies' Advertising Excellence award for his team's presentation to Levi Strauss and Foot, Cone and Belding's senior management group. The presentation was a competition amongst Northern California advertising and marketing professionals (six teams of 6-8 each) who were given the task of preparing a marketing plan for the soon to be introduced Levi's Dockers. Mark's team was declared the winner. Much of the strategy from that marketing and merchandising plan was used by Levi Strauss for its number one selling brand in the Company's history.

From the advertising agency business, Mark worked in the gourmet food sector as a brand manager for Honey Hill Farms. Mark was responsible for launching the company's super premium frozen yogurt which targeted Haagen Dazs in the upscale pint category. He quickly learned the consumer packaged goods business while working with the company's ad agency, overseeing a national sampling program, presenting the marketing plan with the sales team at key chain meetings and assisting/recommending R & D on new flavor introductions.

After Honey Hill Farms, Mark went to work for the British Trade and Investment Office (BTIO). His background in food and beverage helped him secure this highly sought after international position. While with the British, Mark earned the status of, "lead post" on food and drink in the

United States for his marketing plan prepared for a prominent Scotch whisky distiller. He enjoyed working for the British for seven years, ultimately reporting to Sir Alistair Hunter, while gaining expertise in the beverage industry. In those seven years he worked with many brewers, cider companies and distilleries. Mark was also a speaker at London's International Food Exhibition (IFE) where he presented his published reports on the US Food and Beverage sectors. Mark was also interviewed live for his research on the US hard cider industry by the British Broadcasting Corporation (BBC) at their studios in London, England.

Once his contract was up with the British, Mark worked several years for Earthgrains calling on Safeway as their Brand Champion, Category and Account Manager. After Earthgrains was purchased by Sara Lee (now Jimmy Dean), Mark joined the powerful beer distributor, Golden Brands, later purchased by DBI, located in South San Francisco, California.

Mark has worked for Golden Brands and DBI for nearly thirteen years as their Marketing Manager. At DBI, Mark manages a brand team, is responsible for a variety of brands as well as the company's special events that are executed in both San Francisco and San Mateo Counties. Mark enjoys the pace and the variety which can range from launching a new micro/craft brand to devising a creative sales incentive program around an international beer brand's marketing plan.

More recently, Mark was invited to participate in Boston Beer Company's, "Brewing the American Dream" competition for beverage entrepreneurs. Mark acted as a "marketing coach" for a variety of companies that attended the June 2013 and May 2014 events held in San Francisco, California.

Mark also has twelve years of adjunct professor experience teaching Marketing and Advertising at both the undergraduate and graduate levels. He has also been published by the American Marketing Association for his article on Guerilla Marketing in the food and beverage industry. Mark is also proud of his football coaching days when he coached with former teammates and had two undefeated seasons with two players ultimately playing pro football.

His passion and fascination for beer dates back to the 1980's when he had one of the largest beer bottle collections anywhere. Unfortunately he ran out of shelf space (that endless quandary!) and his parents made him take the colorful assortment down.

From his first taste of Pabst Blue Ribbon as a teenager (shhhh) he was hooked on beer and continues to love the category, the passion and the people within it.

DEDICATION

This book is dedicated to my dad, Ron Colburn, who helped me greatly with my marketing education and my grandfather, Ken Colburn, who taught me the importance of relationship building in business and how that translates into sales. I must also thank my darling fiancé, Starla, for her support over these four long years of writing and for her editing of the book. Thanks also to Kim, Rob and Kevin for your helpful input!

TABLE OF CONTENTS

i - PREFACE

This book is intended to assist the small to medium craft brewer with marketing, sales and distribution questions on how to succeed in the US beverage industry. It will also be of value to beverage professionals and recent college graduates who are curious to learn more about consumer packaged goods marketing, sales and distribution. I have written the book based on my own educational and professional training and experiences in the field, citing these continuously throughout the book.

My style is based on a funnel principle whereby I begin at the top with broad based overviews such as market size and trends then spiral down to the bottom with specific examples and recommendations. I hope you will enjoy and benefit from my experience and recommendations. I say this with a caveat in that I do not guarantee that my recommendations will work for your specific company as all situations are different and require tailored marketing plans to fit a company's nuances and competitive situation.

Many brewers today are introducing new styles and style off-shoots at a lightning-fast-pace. This over segmentation of the market leads to product cannibalism which is a marketing term referring to manufacturers who produce two (or more) very similar products that meet one consumer need yet require the support of two marketing budgets. It is strongly suggested, therefore, that prior to brewing or distilling a new product some research and rationale are provided to support this expensive introduction even before the R & D phase begins.

Although it may seem like a good thing to do at the time, consideration should be taken into account for buyer response (they will quickly become jaded by the constant flow of "me too" products if sales teams continue to hound them with products that are not significantly different from the current line up and that are not appropriate to their customer base), wholesaler capacity, incentive support, the sales process required from your team, tap handle cannibalism/trade out and overall marketing resources. From a consumer's perspective, with each product that you send to the market with marginal differentiation from the others, you risk consumer brand dissociation as the consumer connection gets lost with each ensuing SKU. This book will help you to better understand how to compete at all levels within the beer business as well as improve your wholesaler selection criteria and relationships.

The US Beer Industry is experiencing its greatest renaissance in the history of the business. In fact a January 2014 report by Judy Hong with Goldman Sachs reported the following key trends supporting this resurgence[1].

> 1-The core beer drinker is coming back.
> 2-Millenials may return to beer as the beer industry closes the gap with wine and spirits. It seems that the finicky millennial appreciates beer's variety and expanding flavor styles.
> 3-Beer's pricing when compared to wine and spirits is also closing.
> 4-The alcohol consumer is noticing beer industry innovation, particularly at the high end.
> 5-US demographics are swinging in favor of beer.
> 6-2015 volume growth is forecasted at 2% and is expected to continue through 2020[2].

The Brewer's Association based in Boulder, Colorado, is a non-profit organization that helps to serve the growth and substantiation of the US craft beer industry. Their purpose statement is, "to promote and protect

American craft brewers, their beers and the community of brewing enthusiasts." The following data, although it may age after this book's publication, is provided to share the overriding positive outlook for sustained optimism for the craft industry. I think it safe to say that forecasts like this will be applicable to craft, spirits, and wines as well, as American consumers continue to gravitate to the better consumables available to them. So what is happening in this white hot industry?

Brewer's Association (BA) economist, Bart Watson, reported in his April, 2015 State of the Industry overview that total beer category dollar sales exceeded $100 billion in 2013 which translates into 196,241,321 barrels of beer (one barrel yields 31 gallons). Further, there were 3,418 breweries in the United States with 2,051 breweries in the planning stages. This total consists of 1,412 brewpubs, 1,871 micros and 135 regional crafts. Only 46 closings! This is the highest number of breweries since the 1880s with 1.7 opening per day[3]. For historical perspective, there were 2,685 breweries in 1876, 357 in 1952, 229 in 1960, 154 in 1970 and 79 in 1982[4]. California alone has over 430 breweries with more popping up weekly.

Some analysts predict 5,000 breweries will be opened by the end of 2015, representing an all-time United States record. Some reports show that there are over 100 new craft or specialty beer companies entering the market – every month. To say that the industry is robust would be leaving some beer on the table as craft beer volume increased a "Godzillian" 18% to 22,200,000 barrels for a total beer share of 1.6%[5].

As a percentage of beer category growth, craft was 6.5% by volume yet 11.9% by dollar share in 2012. At the close of 2013, the BA reported that craft volume share, of all beer, grew to 7.8% and by a whopping 14.3% dollar share to over $14 billion. In 2014, volume grew again to 11% on 19.3% dollar share. This performance is truly impressive within the food and drink industry and is expected to reach as high as 20% by 2020 per the Brewer's Association[6].

In Mr. Benj Steinman's April, 2014 presentation at the Craft Brewer's Conference in Denver, Colorado, his numbers were even more optimistic as he revealed how the craft beer category has grown 80% from 2008 to 2013 despite the beer industry being down 4% during the same time span - losing share to spirits and wine. Speaking about the On Premise, Mr. Steinman shared that one-third of all dollars spent in this channel were attributed to craft beer purchases. Interestingly, in bars, hotels and restaurants, over 1,000 new craft brands were introduced to the On Premise. The craft category also contributed to increasing patron check averages by 15%. The most robust craft growth On Premise was in fine dining which was up 13%, with bars up 11% and casual up 7%.In 2014, Mr. Steinman forecasts the craft category to maintain double digit growth at 15% as more consumers gravitate to better quality beers[7].

It is important here to define exactly what is - a craft brewer? The BA has altered this definition slightly in 2015 to the following: "An American craft brewer is small, independent and traditional." The Association further defines the craft brewer below[8].

Small: Annual production of 6 million barrels of beer or less (approximately 3 percent of U.S. annual sales). Beer production is attributed to the rules of alternating proprietorships.

Independent: Less than 25 percent of the craft brewery is owned or controlled (or equivalent economic interest) by an alcoholic beverage industry member that is not itself a craft brewer.

Traditional: A brewer that has a majority of its total beverage alcohol volume in beers whose flavor derives from traditional or innovative brewing ingredients and their fermentation. Flavored malt beverages (FMBs) are not considered beers[8].

So why the explosion in craft brewing? There are multiple reasons. The most significant is the consumer taste switch from domestic beer to craft and albeit a smaller percentage, to imports. It seems that domestic drinkers are using amber and/or Hefeweizen craft styles as stepping stones into the craft segment then graduating to pale, "session able IPAs," IPA, stouts, porters, sours and others. The second major reason is the growth in the 21-34 year old demographic, known as the Millennial. With 57 million Millennial drinkers today, there is much optimism in the industry as this group is expected to expand to 81 million by 2020[9]. This segment is not concerned about brand loyalty. They want the best products and they want them now.

Another long term trend, also enjoyed by the spirits and wine categories is the trade up to higher quality beverages. This drink-less-but-better philosophy began with the baby boomers (78 million in the US) as they realized their days of polishing off a full bottle of spirits or wine or even a couple of six packs were long over. With the country's highest discretionary income and education levels, the 'boomers bought into marketing pitches for upscale wine, scotch, tequila, vodka...and most certainly for craft and imported beers. Watch for this trend of buying better but consuming less to continue.

Premiumization – Get a Little Less of the Good Stuff

Paul Gatza agrees with the drink better long term trend stating that he sees, "an imminent share shift towards the high end." Moreover, the beverage alcohol high end segment grew 1 share point in 2011 which included crafts and imports. Paul estimates this segment at 12 share points when high end spirits and wine are included which bodes well for super premium craft and import brands[10].

These short and long term trends bode well for brewers, however, there may be some grey clouds in the lager. The issue for so many brewers is; where are they all going to fit? Are there enough distributors to get the beers to market? Is there adequate retail space to properly merchandise all these great brands? Will you settle for the warm shelf? How will your local sports bar make the decision to carry brand "X's" IPA on draft vs. brand "Y" or "Z" or "A" or "B"? Brand and SKU proliferation is not rampant – it will be epidemic. And how will thirsty consumers make their purchase decisions?

Bump Williams, beverage alcohol consultant on the industry stated in a January 2014 state of the industry address, that retailers only want brands that produce (i.e., sell). In fact, many are beginning to evaluate brands by their price per ounce vs. velocity per ounce. After they do this retailers plan to study which beer segments and packages are truly generating the profit and growth needed by the large retail chains.

With over 10,000 beer packages in the United States, a SKU shakeout is inevitable. This will result in big brand package cuts (currently taking up "dead real estate") as retailers realize that they do not need to carry a six pack, twelve pack, fifteen pack, 24 ounce single serve, three pack, eighteen pack, thirty-pack and conventional twenty-four pack case all of the same brand. They are also realizing that this brand bias results in out of stocks for more popular craft beers that may have just one slot for either their six packs or 22-24 ounce bomber bottle.

Another interesting point made by Mr. Williams was that retailers are now looking at a new data point, "items not handled." This report includes a list of "hot" items that retailers do not currently carry but realize they need to make space for. This is a list to be on – for the short term. These changes to the retail side of the business are very promising to the craft brewer, especially for the ones that brew popular styles such as IPAs (West Coast and Imperial) and sour Belgian style beers.

So what does the passionate brewer do with his/her prized liquid offspring? They may hire equally talented marketing and sales people to market their beer, merge with other brewers (watch for some big announcements...), consider contract brewing or go bankrupt. With so many great beers looming on the retail horizon each vying for premium yet scarce real estate, door closure for some will be inevitable. There just isn't space nor are there enough quality distributors to handle this onslaught.

You probably are thinking that your beer is so much better than anyone else's and that you won't have this dilemma. Don't let your ego blind you. The key to success is investment. You will need a solid marketing manager or consultant, feet on the street and a comprehensive marketing strategy supported by committed distributor partners. You will also need to "out market" the others. This book will help show you why you must do this.

If you believe that the beer industry will go through a shakeout due to over segmentation resulting in too many brands competing for single privations, then you should buy this book. A shakeout or shake up seems imminent despite the increasing quality level of brews available to American consumers. That may be unfortunate for those who have space. However, retailers just won't be able to stomach product cannibalism as their category managers will be hard at work divvying out space to only the strongest and best marketed brands.

If you do not understand these terms or what marketing really is, then you should buy this book. If you are a craft, import or domestic brewer, either a veteran or newbie, then you should buy this book. If you are affiliated with the spirits or wine business, then you should buy this book as it will provide you with ideas on how to market your brands as well as how to better manage the shrinking distributor/wholesaler pool.

A trend for you to monitor is beer distributors stepping into wine and/or expanding their licenses to distribute spirits. Why are they doing this? Because the few, large spirits and wine wholesalers do not share love with small to medium-sized brands. Will the huge wine distributors be able to warehouse and sell the growing draft bourbon and wine brands? I doubt it. Do they have the personnel to do this? And these niche, high-end categories are precisely where the millennial likes to play, and 'boomers like to discover.

If you are a graduating senior who abhors the high tech sector as much as I do and you are considering joining the beverage industry then you, too, should buy this book. If you are a marketing professor who wants to add some extra credit reading to his/her class on an "old school" subject, then you should recommend this book to your university. If you are in the non-alcoholic beverage business then this book is for you too as it serves as a catalyst for ideas that you can combine with your own for some highly creative marketing execution. It will also teach you a great deal about US beverage distribution. If you are an MBA with marketing responsibility and little time for creativity but an interest in ascending the ladder, then this book is also for you. Lastly, if you are a European or International agency looking to learn more about how the US market works on behalf of your exporters, then this would be a valuable book to disseminate prior to the execution of their export program, joint venture or market visit. Herbologists? You can learn a great deal about how to market your adult-herbs as well. So please read on.

DSD Definition

Before we get into the hops of this book, let us first be sure that we understand how most alcoholic and many non alcoholic beverages get to their final On and Off Premise locations. On Premise is hereby defined as bars, nightclubs, restaurants, hotels/motels, lounges, bowling alleys, golf courses, delis and sporting venues. This is where beverage alcohol can be consumed at the point of purchase in either draft or packaged (bottle or can) formats. Off Premise, referred to as the General Market, Independents or Up and Down the Street class of trade includes corner markets, supermarkets, wholesale clubs, convenience stores (referred to as C-Stores), gas stations, drug chains, liquor stores and chain grocery stores.

The term "DSD" stands for Direct Store Delivery. This form of distribution requires a wholesaler/distributor (these terms are used interchangeably throughout the book) to physically receive beer or alcohol from the supplier (brewer, vineyard, distillery, etc.). The distributor warehouses the product and then physically takes it to the final selling location such as an Off Premise retailer or an On Premise bar/nightclub/hotel/restaurant – provided they possess the necessary license to resell the beverages. This three-way process is known as the Three Tier Law.

Three Tier Law - Defined

In 1919 the US Congress passed the 18th Amendment totally outlawing the manufacture, distribution and sales of alcoholic beverages. This dark period in our history quickly became known as the "Prohibition Era" which stimulated illegal alcohol sales spawning the emergence of "moonshine runners" that replaced the services offered by wholesalers. However, in 1932, Franklin Delano Roosevelt entered the Presidential race as a Democrat. His claim (or "KDA") to the Presidency was the end of Prohibition and the return to "wet traditions." After his election, the 21st Amendment was passed (party time!) by Congress in fewer than one hundred days, bringing an end to Prohibition. The newly ratified amendment returned to the states the power over the sale and distribution of beer, wine and spirits. This resulted in Federal and State tax levies as well as eradication of the "tied house" (see Federal Alcohol Act – 1933) which forbade anti-competitive arrangements within the Nation's three-tier system. (Source: Wikipedia).

Two models emerged from the 21st Amendment as states were allowed to creatively interpret the Amendment. Thirty-two states (including California) opted to permit the private sector to distribute and sell alcoholic beverages (including DSD). The remaining eighteen decided to adopt a "control model" whereby the state is involved in one or more tiers of the three-tier system. The following graphic depicts the traditional 3-tier system as practiced for over 70 years by the 32 US states[11].
(Illustrations taken from Clip Art files, black and white photo taken from Google Images public library).

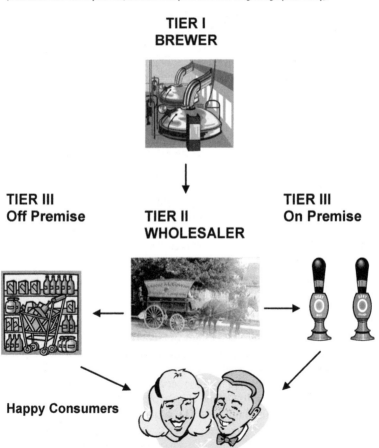

TIER I
BREWER

TIER III
Off Premise

TIER II
WHOLESALER

TIER III
On Premise

Happy Consumers

The three-tier law benefits states and consumers in many ways. It essentially establishes a series of checks and balances requiring specific tiers to be held accountable for valuable aspects of the process. Here are a few benefits of the law:

1-Minors do not have access to alcohol.

2-Taxes are collected and remitted to state and local governments.

3-Quality control is ensured for those 21 and over.

4-A level playing field is created between small and large retailers thus promoting competitive market health.

5-It establishes a clear chain of accountability.

Craft Brewer Categories

I see the craft beer business as comprised of six categories.

Mini Micro – Just graduated from home brewing and actively selling via self-distribution. Typical barrelage will not exceed 100 per year. A barrel is defined as 31 US gallons.

Nano Micro – Still self-distributing but adding some smaller distributors along the way. Barrelage loosely defined as 101-2,500 barrels per year.

Local Craft – Getting traction with some local distributors (you sold the self-distribution truck). This could also include brew pubs/restaurants that sell to the public and to nearby distributors. Defined as a Local Craft brewer that produces between 2,501- 15,000 barrels annually.

Regional Craft – Brew 15,001 – 200,000 barrels and distributes brand(s) throughout a number of regional states. The brand(s), however, do not have national distribution.

National Craft – Full-fledged brewery/ies with the majority of US metro markets covered via DSD distribution. Barrelage is defined as producing between 200,001 - 6,000,000 barrels annually.

Multi National Factory Brewer – International brewer that leverages/exploits this efficiency. Often dominates all preceding categories by sheer size. Barrelage requirement exceeds 6,000,001 barrels annually. Company is also publicly traded on globally recognized stock exchanges.

I – **M**arketing, Why Bother?

I recall a lively conversation with a petroleum engineer working for one of the largest gasoline refiners in the world. She stated that marketing simply adds to the cost of her fuels which results in higher prices to the end consumer. She firmly believed that by eliminating expensive marketing personnel that she could help make the company more profitable while reducing the price per gallon to the consumer, ultimately improving the brand's competitiveness in the marketplace. I asked her where I could buy her company's fuel. She gave me quite a look as the fuels were available at most major intersections throughout the country. I then asked how the final price per gallon was determined (with its resultant effect on the brand) and how do consumers know about the new SU2000 Super Unleaded fuel that she was responsible for introducing throughout the country? She smirked and said to go to my local gas station to get a fill up and learn about the new SU2000 by picking up a brochure at the station or by watching a TV ad during a NASCAR race (which featured their sponsored car) or to ask the gas station owner about pricing.

I explained that marketing is responsible for how the fuel gets to the station, where the stations are located, the station design and layout, how the fuel is priced and what media are used, such as TV and NASCAR sponsorship to create consumer awareness for the product. Further, I told her that marketing is behind the name, SU2000, and without such; her fuel would be perceived as a commodity and that consumers would not know where to buy it. I also explained that the materials available to the station owner and then disseminated to consumers were created by her marketing department. She reluctantly began to understand the role of marketing and its contribution to building a high quality brand with which consumers could trust and try when her team introduced new products – such as SU2000. The moral here is, do not make assumptions in areas where you have no credibility and do not underestimate the power and significance of marketing.

As a brewer, vintner, or distiller, you may think a lot like the engineer, as you will expect consumers to immediately know about your great line of beers, wine or bourbon – and in turn to buy them from you. The objective reality is that the market is filled with thousands of products entering the market every year. Some reports forecast that there will be as many as 4,000 craft beer SKUs available in the US. These great products all vie for consumer attention, trial and ultimately, purchase or as we say in marketing, share of stomach. So how does a consumer wake up Monday morning and learn about your great brands? Through the marketing mix.

What is Marketing's Role?

Having worked in the marketing field for nearly thirty years I have seen the escalation of financial accountability on marketing's behalf. Long gone are the days of one and two minute television ads and actual advertising campaigns that invested much needed equity into brands that created "brand personality." These campaigns, now a thing of the past, built mighty brands, some of which still stand strong today. In the past fifteen to twenty years, however, stockholders have begun to demand immediate financial results from the marketing team holding them accountable to goals once relegated to the sales organization.

Back in the seventies and eighties, the marketing team created the marketing plan for the sales team to execute at field level. Nowadays, the marketing role is blending with that of the sales function – moving away from staff to line status within the corporation. This unfortunate trend signals the end to classic branding strategy, which takes time (years or even decades) and resources (repetitive investment). Stockholders, however, have little patience for the latter.

So what is marketing's role going forward? Novices immediately blurt out "sales," however; sales are the by-product of a solid marketing program. Marketing is tasked with the definition of wants and needs relevant to the sponsoring company's offering, the quantification and identification of a target market and the delivery of want/need satisfying goods or services to that receptive target audience. So how does a company satisfy these needs? Through the successful blending of the Marketing Mix, which is the first half of a company's marketing strategy.

The classical Marketing Mix consists of the, "Four P's." The most emphasized of these includes product, price and promotion. The latter oftentimes receives the bulk of press as it includes high profile investments including advertising, sales promotion, sampling, Internet/social media and public relations. This book, however, will focus on the, "upside down P."

The Most Important "P"

After graduate school I went into the advertising agency business landing a position as a marketing research analyst. I worked on some really slick campaigns and saw how the big agencies pitched accounts. In addition, I learned about marketing plans and how agencies exploit the promotion (i.e. advertising) side of those plans. It surprised me to see how many companies did not actually take the time to prepare an annual marketing plan. This act of laziness represented an open door to our Ivy-League educated senior Vice Presidents looking to sell the client a fat TV ad deal. I then went to the supplier side as a brand manager and got to manage the advertising agency and rather liked it. I prepared our marketing plan which included TV, FSIs (free standing inserts or Sunday coupons), a national demo program, radio, coupons and more.

What I realized was, that with all this great planning, TV ads, demos, coupons, award-winning packaging, radio and product research, a brand was dead in the water if it did not have first class distribution to get it to market. This was assumed by my peers as an afterthought – and naively by us. Perhaps a misnomer from the eighties and nineties, I learned a lifelong lesson, and that was:

Marketing Corollary #1: *Never assume distribution for your brand.*

I vividly recall going into distributor presentations after we had paid for the advertising on The Tonight Show and Letterman and booked the FSI drops with demos in major markets. As a new brand, we had pre-spent millions of marketing dollars. Fortunately we were able to convince most of the distributors in our markets to take on our brand, but by doing so in reverse order, we jeopardized everything. Back then, distribution was assumed and considered automatic. "How could these clowns turn down the plans we have for this brand?" I recall our Senior Vice President of Sales asking in a strategy meeting. The better route to have taken would have been be to have presented to the large supermarket chains, procured schematic authorization and THEN present to the distributors covering those chains and key retailers, so vital to the success of our brand.

THE most important thing that you can do for your brand is to create a sound distribution model or "foot print" so that consumers can try and hopefully buy your beverages. Remember that you can have the best ad agency, the most outstanding IPA ever to cross your lips, the coolest logo, the most fairly priced product and/or the slickest web site ever created but without distribution your brand will fail miserably.

Distribution is THE most important element within your brand's marketing mix. I never thought that I would work at a distributor as they were looked upon as the bottom of the marketing/sales barrel – but after working at one for over a decade now, I can't over emphasize the importance of a solid distribution channel partner. Distribution, or what I call the upside down "P" is the most important element to your brand's

A

success and you <u>must</u> prioritize this crucial channel accordingly. Once in place, you can properly begin to grow your brand to its fullest potential.

NEXT STEP - Identifying and Pursuing Your Target Market

Before getting into this critical area of your marketing strategy, read Professor Philip Kotler's interview response to the question: *"What are the points that a CMO (Chief Marketing Officer) must remember before setting a marketing plan?"*

> **Philip Kotler:** "The first need is to get each marketing planner to carefully define the target audience and deeply understand their needs and desires and the main triggers to purchase. The aim should be to discover something new about that target audience, some new insight into their psyche that will cause them to want to take the offer"[12].

After identifying the marketing mix from within the marketing plan, the second half of the marketing strategy is the definition of the target market. Remember that the underlying purpose of marketing is to satisfy consumer wants and needs. These needs are the center, or focal point, of all marketing activity. Once you know what your consumer wants, then you can satisfy those needs with superior quality liquids. But who do you produce for? Where are they located? What do they look for in a quality beer, spirit or wine? What you must do next is identify and clearly define the target audience for your products, and then pursue them via the successful manipulation of marketing mix variables.

So, who is your target market? In most US states that answer will begin with adults who are over 21 years of age, assuming that you produce an alcoholic product. Is your work done? Not even close. The next step is to identify or *segment* the market into slices appropriate to your brands. The Boston Beer Company does this exceptionally well. In a presentation made in San Francisco, Boston Beer executives shared their take on how the beer market is segmented. You'll see below how they perceive the US beer market. The terms refer to consumers who drink beer as a total category.

Casual – 35%, Core – 52%, Heavy – 13% and Geek – 2%.

Further defining the beer category by paring it down to craft/micros reveals which segments purchase and consume the most craft beer.

Casual – 13%, Core – 62%, Heavy/Geek – 25%

Profile

The purpose of the above example is to familiarize the reader on how target markets can be divided or segmented for marketing purposes. What is happening in the beer industry is many domestic beer drinkers are stepping into the craft beer segment while import drinkers, seeking more flavorful beers, are doing the same. There is research available that estimates even further the target audience segments by beer styles. Once you have an estimate of the total number of craft drinkers in your market, you can then decide if that geography warrants brand pursuit/investment.

What I found most useful from my ad agency days was going through the exercise of profiling the most typical consumer for my client's product then sharing this with our creative teams. I strongly suggest doing this so that you and ALL of your relevant partners (wholesaler, sales team, retailers, etc.) have a crystal clear understanding of who is your primary target audience. The more you learn about this group the more successful you will be. This takes work and not many companies or employees want to expend the effort which can lead to a competitive advantage for you.

Let us build a profile for an example, something that is done to accompany the creative strategy during ad campaign development. Here is the scenario: We own a small brewery in the southwest, competition is escalating but not as significant as in other major geographies like Colorado, Northern and Southern California or the Eastern seaboard. We have been brewing for just under two years selling to the local clientele. Here is who we understand to be our primary target consumer:

— "Austin"*

Age: 29, defined as Millennial (estimated at ninety-five million in the US, sixty million are legal drinking age),

Target Range: 21-39, twenty-five percent of microbrew drinkers are between the ages of 30-39. By 2023, half of all craft drinkers will be Millennials, consuming an estimated 65% of beer volume.

Education: Bachelor's Degree

Sex: Male

Employment: Employed Full Time, skews middle management, high tech or engineering position, fifty-four percent of craft drinkers are white collar.

Marital Status: Single

Household Size: 1-2

Ethnicity: Caucasian or other

Geography: West Coast, East Coast, Southern Belt, Pacific Northwest, no geographic dominance, however, skews metro area

Residence: Rented

Residence Location: Metro as opposed to suburban location

Household Income: $65,000 per annum

Automotive Situation: Owns own car or relies on public transit

Psychographic Makeup: Relishes time with friends, active on weekends, attends minimum of one concert or live music event per month, attends minimum of one professional sports event per month, exercises 3-4 times per week in gym or is active playing weekend sports with friends, goes out to dinner which includes consuming alcohol once-twice per week, enjoys better brands when entertaining including the purchase of craft beers, attends movie theatres a minimum of 1-2 times per month, enjoys playing poker with friends once per month. A whopping 80% of Millennials hear about products through word of mouth.

Media Habits: Voracious consumer of all social media as well as high frequency internet participation. Compulsive listener of music via multiple outlets available to him. Spend over twenty hours per week surfing the Web. Key brand gatekeeper/opinion leader that has power to influence friend community of over three hundred. Is also influenced by social media input and is constantly looking to discover new brands and experiences. Demands constant entertainment from social media to the point of addiction. Minimalist television viewing with the exception of live sports broadcasts and cable programming. Shuns television commercials feeling they are deceptive and a waste of time.

Buying Style: Characterized as impulsive and promiscuous. Brand loyalty is very difficult to achieve and to sustain within this target audience. This target audience is loyal to quality and thrives on experimentation.

Product Adoption Stage: Innovator-Early adopter, actively seeks out what is new so that he can influence and impress his social media "cyber clan." Austin remains engaged with products through experimentation, particularly at the higher end of the product price spectrum. As a result, he demands more, different and better.

Beer Consumption: Medium to heavy. This target actively looks for craft beer in their favorite bars. Nearly one-third of this target likes to try or discover beer at bars (On Premise). If they like the beer there is a sixty percent likelihood that they will purchase that brand Off Premise. Over half of craft beer dollar volume comes from On Premise bar purchases.

Conventional Media: Subscribes to 1-2 magazines per month

Other: Dog or pet owner

As you can see from our fictitious profile you get a real feel for Austin as your primary consumer of your southwestern-brewed beer. Once you get a clear definition of your base audience then you can tailor your marketing plan around him/her. By approaching the market in this fashion you will reduce risk and improve the likelihood of success in the marketplace[13].

*Profile style taken from author's marketing presentation made to Levi's Dockers Sr Mgt. and Foote, Cone and Belding, May 5, 1988 pgs. 5-6.

Marketing Corollary #2: *The greater the find - the more friends that will share in the bounty.*
When it comes to the craft beer consumer, focus group moderators (a focus group is a form of qualitative marketing research that is led by a moderator who asks for feedback on something like a flavor profile or advertising concept from eight-ten gatekeepers or high category brand or product users based on usage frequency) will tell you that drinkers want to "discover" new brands and styles in their favorite bars or retailers Pairing adequate distribution to these brand-appropriate accounts will help increase the probability that your target market will find your brand. Try to get into that consumer's mindset objectively and think of it as their fun escape from their boring routine as they go on your brand treasure hunt.

You can begin to see the importance of distribution and target market definition as they work together to help you build your brand.

II- THE PRODUCT LIFE CYCLE and WHY ITS DEFINITION IS CRUCIAL TO YOUR BRAND'S SURVIVAL

Many magazine and newspaper articles as well as blogs mention or reference the product life cycle, but few, if any, explain its relevance or application. I sometimes wonder if these writers really understand just what a product life cycle is and how it relates to marketing strategy, the target market, and the, "Four Ps." Marketers often define the brand's selling span of existence as the Product Life Cycle. To be sure you are clear on this important facet of your brand let us establish a precise definition of such going forward. According to Professor Philip Kotler, the classical product life cycle is divided into four distinct stages. As you will see, each stage has a different bearing on marketing strategy selection and management. The first stage is the Introduction phase, the second, Growth, the third, Maturity, the final stage, Decline[14].

Each stage of the cycle should be carefully managed by your marketing team as brand health will be dictated by how well it is managed through each of these stages. Your marketing team will be responsible for when and what "marketing vitamins" need to be taken/applied throughout the brand maturation process. Although identifying in which stage your brand resides is not a simple process, the easiest way to graph this cycle is to map time (X axis) over sales (Y axis). In the Introduction phase, the beverage marketer begins with a new product that the trade and consumer most likely know little, if anything about. As a brewer in the craft business, you may have just started brewing your new line of beers. Executing the appropriate marketing elements in this first phase is critical to the brand's success. Here is where great emphasis and strict dedication must be followed.

Intro – The Birth of the Brand, TRIAL is the Name of the Game!

The marketing recipe during the Introduction stage of the product life cycle (PLC) must emphasize <u>distribution</u> and be supported by consumer and trade trial and awareness generation as a result of the marketing team's efforts. This may seem like common sense but you would be amazed at what companies will spend on a product launch despite not having distribution in a market. Newly launched brands in the Introduction stage should be supported with product demos/samplings in relevant retail OR On Premise locations so that your target audience can try your brand. Remember Austin? Where legal, a coupon or price discount can help influence that first purchase and is strongly recommended.

When investing in demos be sure to educate your sampling team with a well prepared message so that this gets communicated exactly as stated in the launch strategy. You may choose to have your KDA (Key Differentiating Advantage) verbalized to every consumer that tastes your product as well as a statement about retail availability. The festivals, where many brewers, vintners, and distillers spend their weekends, can be a great venue to do this work. Some consumers, especially beer and wine lovers, will have detailed questions which should be anticipated and prepared for so that the demonstrator/server/bartender can react on the spot with accurate brand information. To impress upon you how important it is to get firmly on base during this stage of the PLC, I will share with you a valuable learning experience.

Consumers do not wake up on a random Monday morning thinking about your beverage. There are thousands of new products that compete for consumer attention each and every year, all vying for share of stomach, and share of fridge. The failure rate for new products in the food and beverage industry is about eighty percent. Because of these odds, brands need to be built in a particular sequence. Please remember that brands, particularly in the introduction stage, require trial and sampling so that consumers can discover your product while expending little if any risk trying them. This is exactly what was needed when I was on the brand team at Honey Hill Farms during our launch of the first ever super premium frozen yogurt.

As the brand's Product Manager, I had the responsibility of managing a large (thousands) product-sampling program (referred to as "demos"). I was excited to be on this team and to take on the goliaths; Haagen Dazs, Frusen Gladje, Steve's and Ben & Jerry's in the super-premium, sixteen-ounce frozen ice cream segment. Part of my job during the launch was to "best spend" a decent sized marketing budget for this western US-distributed brand. The brand was in the Introduction stage of the product life cycle and I knew I had my work cut out against well entrenched competitors with huge marketing budgets.

Some of the first steps I took were to interview, then hire a large sampling agency that could handle supermarket demo waves of three to five hundred per weekend. I then spent four weekends in a row travelling to various stores throughout the state of California just "being a consumer" and observing trends in multiple food and drink categories. As I walked the large supermarkets, I noted how the giant consumer product companies did little, if anything, to train their demonstrators that served their products to the thousands of prospective customers. I was appalled at the number of demonstrators that simply said, "Here you go" presenting sponsor brands in a commodity-like approach. My research revealed an exploitable competitor weakness. They were much bigger than us, so they ignored the demonstrator as potential brand ambassador, seeing them more as a product handout tool or "granny robot."

Armed with these findings I returned to the office to prepare a demonstrator training package with complete instructions on how to present the brand and how to conduct *my* demo. Included in the large kit was a branded apron, nutritional information, branded serving tray, empty pints, serving spoons, cups, photo of the "perfect demo configuration" and tablecloth as well as a comprehensive demonstrator manual that provided answers to as many potential questions that interested consumers might ask. I topped this off with significant value coupons, a demonstrator "mystery shopper," and a sales volume incentive. The latter two items were new to the large demo agency (this was in the late eighties) and the response was Herculean.

Before the demos were executed I knew that we could not rely on the demonstrators physically reading and retaining all the information in my training kit. Having a creative mind and coming from the advertising agency business, I decided to "direct and produce" the company's first ever video to visually and creatively promote the brand. Instead of showing a huge factory spewing out frozen yogurt into little pint containers, I told a story (brand script) that took quite a bit of creative license.

After preparing a creative strategy for the video I went to a library. There I found historic black and white photos of California from the 1800's that included old dairy wagons pulled by horses. I copied these and super imposed our logo into each. I then crafted a fun and somewhat zany story about the brand and how it came to be. Remember to make it fun so people will watch and remember. I knew the video would need to be short (less than ten minutes) and ended it upbeat with the three key salient points to be communicated in mass to our potential customers during the supermarket demos. These points took a great deal of time to determine and then prioritize.

My boss, a former Dole Products executive, felt that communicating the fact that the product was yogurt was good enough to convince consumers to buy our healthy product over Haagen Dazs, Frusen Gladje, Steve's and Ben & Jerry's. I knew we needed more ammo to convince these long-time ice cream fanatics to try our frozen yogurt that as a category was often perceived as being too tart or sour. One night while working very late trying to decide what my "demo army" would say to each and every consumer, I had on my desk thirty or so empty pint cartons from our competitors as well as ours.

It then struck me to read all of the pint container's fine print, searching for a significant marketing clue to use for my fledgling brand. After reading all the competitive flowery copy, I dug into the nutritional information dividing it back into their stated serving sizes. Through all the numbers I determined that our product was exactly half the fat and one-third the calories of Haagen Dazs! That was a cool marketing chink in the armor moment as the clock ticked past midnight. From that point on, this was the first thing out of every demonstrator's mouth. I felt as though we had won the marketing lotto that night.

Once the video editing was done and the kits completed, I went on "brand tour" to present the product line and our company to my demo army. My goal was to convert each and every one of them into passionate, educated and professional brand ambassadors in essence, "mini Marks," and to provide something entertaining that the demonstrators would remember. The video was then mass produced and used to educate the legions of demonstrators hired to present our brand in major US supermarkets. I knew, however, that simply shipping the video to their regional managers would not provide the results that we, as a tiny company, needed to make this brand building investment pay for itself.

To dot the "I"s, I made multiple presentations to these demonstrators in large venues (high school auditoriums) where we could sample the product, give them a coupon for a free pint to eat at home, show the video, answer questions and go over the incentive while imparting my brand passion and DNA into each member of the audience. Dozens and dozens of these demonstrators told me personally that no company had ever gone to this effort before. I could see the appreciation in their eyes, they were captivated by the presentation but perhaps more by the attention and respect directed towards them. I knew I was onto something when I realized while walking the many supermarkets during my research that the "big boys" took the demonstrator "grannies" for granted. Therein was their chink in the armor. From that point on, we owned "Granny Nation" and I will say, when you have granny on eight cylinders, she is someone to be reckoned with.

Sales Results

After attending many demos during our "demo waves" (which included awarding well-studied demonstrators during my mystery shopper walk-byes), I got to see the sales results first hand. We did not have to wait for Nielsen or IRI data because I had generated a "before and after inventory" tracking sheet included in each kit which the demonstrator filled out (I negotiated this procedure with the demo agency principals) with impressive accuracy. It was made clear, however, that demonstrators would not be paid unless this paper work was completed.

The case sales results were simply unbelievable. The demo company reported that they had never seen so many cases sold of a product in our category in the company's history and, they executed demos for our competition! The supermarket dairy buyers and demo agency managers agreed saying that the demos were the most successful that they had ever seen. To my amazement, there was one gentleman who sold 280 cases (not units) of product during a weekend demo in San Ramon, California. I made sure he worked for us every time we conducted demos anywhere near his residence. What was his secret? He dressed in a tuxedo and took my table preparation concept to a stratospheric level featuring candles, white tablecloth and real silver serving tray. I watched him in action before I introduced myself and applauded his personal selling efforts. He believed that every single consumer that stepped within 10 yards of the frozen foods aisle, came to see him and to buy his/our product(s). He was not pushy, rather he quickly learned from initial conversation what buttons to push once he sized up each of his customers. Naturally he won every volume bonus that we ever created for these teams.

The point to take away is not how well I prepared for this investment. What I want you to see is how great results can be achieved via hard work (including homework) and creativity. This is what it is going to take for your beverage brands to win in the dwindling retail space landscape especially as you compete with long established brand giants. I suspect also, that sampling will become much more widely employed by brewers and beverage companies as more retailers adopt this practice for alcoholic beverages. In fact, in early 2014, warehouse giant Costco executed its first ever alcohol sampling program in six of its warehouses. Supermarket powerhouse Safeway also launched an alcoholic beverage sampling division in 2015. This avenue may be an excellent route to one-up your competition while showing the retail buyer just how well your brand is being received. I suggest that you look into this soon as more retailers are applying for alcoholic product demo licenses.

Some supermarket chains such as Whole Foods are even selling draft craft beer! Try to impart a tiny slice of your brewery at demo-level, like I did with Honey Hill Farms AND don't ever take the person pitching your brand for granted. They are people, too, and want to be treated with respect. In fact, many product demonstrators consider their trade to be a professional occupation. Food and beverage brand teams that do not recognize and appreciate this valuable sales promotion tool will get marginal results (at best) on their investment. Think, too, about the fact that these demonstrators/samplers are CUSTOMERS and have GREAT word of mouth influence with their friends, family AND other demonstrators. In essence, these people are valuable gatekeepers that MUST be converted to your brand ambassadors. You might take this concept to the next level and invite quality demo people to your brewery, winery or distillery just to get them on your side and to spread your brand gospel.

Realize that there is a chink in your competition's armor. It may not be easy to find but as companies get larger, they also have more fronts to attack and to defend. As a small to medium-sized beverage company, it is your marketing team's or consultant's job to find and exploit that weakness. There is a marketing path to success, and the Introduction stage is where you repeatedly apply those learnings such as the experience from my demo program above.

I need you to understand the difference in how I approached the demonstrator as opposed to the how the giant food corporations took them for granted opting not to waste time and resources on them. These people are not mindless sub-contractors, they are your future customers and Brand Ambassadors, hungry to learn about and how to sell your brands. This over-the-top effort is how you will win in your respective markets. The art of creativity mixed with tenacity is waning. Take full advantage of sleeping giants, but be careful to stay below their radar.

On-Premise

There are also great opportunities to sample your alcoholic products in the On Premise (bars, nightclubs, taverns, restaurants, etc.) where consumers enjoy discovering new beverages. This discovery will in turn lead to brand trial which boosts the brand further up its Introduction stage trajectory. Be sure to check with all state laws before you plan alcohol samplings, especially at the retailer level. More specialty retailers, in California for example, are applying for sampling licenses that allow your brand to be consumed on site. This trend will continue (on a trip in Nevada, we visited a warehouse-format alcohol retailer which was conducting no fewer than six alcohol-related product demonstrations!) and expand, so it would be wise to watch for ambassadors who share your brand's passion and leverage their expertise at the On and Off Premise levels. These people are not easy to find and are often snapped up quickly. Once you find them, I suggest that you hire them and set them up in a position whereby they can succeed and flourish within your company.

As stated, gaining initial distribution is imperative, without such, consumers will not be able to learn about or experience (buy) your products. Selecting the appropriate distribution channel is crucial. If you are selling a high end beverage you will not want it sold in a discount mass merchandiser or dollar store outlet. Always remember that your retail channel is a direct reflection upon your brand's quality and image within the mindset of your consumer (target audience).

Growth Stage – Shifting into Second

The Growth stage is a phase where the brand is really generating impressive pull, taking hold, and gaining traction in the marketplace. Characterized by a "howitzer trajectory," volume trends and building distribution gains for key SKUs. This period is where you really "put the gas down" as the Growth stage sets the table for the future success of the brand. In the Growth stage, distribution should be gaining rapidly. In fact, this is where you want to look at expanding into other relevant markets, provided you **can supply, support and afford such**. During this period you will want to hire local and/or regional sales reps to work with distributors in order to better sell your brands. These full time reps will make individual sales calls on key accounts and ride with the distributor's sales force.

The festivals mentioned in the Introduction phase should continue to be invested in as cumulative exposure will only serve the brand well with its target audience. "Oh I remember seeing your brand here last year, it was so good!" As you learn from attending these festivals you'll note the flow that the consumer takes as he/she enters the venue. The first thing they do after getting their drinking vessel is to search out their favorite brands. After "getting a taste of home" from these brands they then continue on their treasure hunt. Repetition at these festivals validates in your consumer's mind that your brand is still highly relevant, new or with it/cool and competitive. It is not good to be noticeably absent from major events that the brand has regularly participated in the past.

At these special events, you can also introduce a new flavor or package as consumers expand their brand familiarity. As your marketing budget grows, sponsorship or co-sponsorship might become an option during the Growth stage which can be leveraged at On and Off Premise buyer level. Retailers appreciate brands that support the community including local festivals which can result in new placements, or in retaining placement when new entrants ask for this space. This community support/investment might just be the difference between staying in an account or being bounced in favor of the new brewer, vintner, or distillery of the month. It can also be used as a competitive key differentiating advantage over a new, threatening brand.

Maturity Stage – Third Gear, How to Maintain the Glow

In the Maturity stage of the Product Life Cycle, volume sales begin to peak while distribution is at its maximum level. At this point, the sales trajectory is plateauing or arcing. It must be said that PLCs for beverages have shrunk dramatically since the sixties and seventies. Many will have their opinions as to why, I will offer mine. In the sixties and seventies, brands were introduced "by the consumer packaged goods book." This meant that substantial resources were spent on advertising which helped to provide a brand equity platform that nourished and allowed brands to grow. Companies like Coke, Lever Brothers, Procter and Gamble, Johnson and Johnson and Clorox used a standard model that included television ads that were at least sixty seconds in length or even as long as two minutes. Radio ads, meanwhile, were also sixty seconds.

As we moved into the mid to late eighties, corporate shareholders got more active in their investments and board meeting participation, demanding quicker returns on their money. This dramatically impacted marketing budgets and strategic execution. The result was marketing plan evolution that emphasized trial via sampling and quick response by the consumer. Media budgets were slashed along with conventional advertising, and brand-building theory. Ads quickly became thirty or even fifteen seconds in length or were scrapped altogether in favor of sampling and couponing programs. This significant change had a rippling impact on brand equity and "substance." Coupled to this trend was a pendulum shift firmly swinging and remaining on the side of the retailer.

As retailer power increased, so did demands for slotting fees (shelf real estate charges) for many categories of consumer goods. This further put the squeeze on marketing budgets, hitting the small companies hardest while forcing large firms to shift dollars from long term brand building to showing positive quarterly results. For those that did not meet investor expectations, they received brand pink slips.

In the Maturity stage, manufacturers, brewers, wineries and distillers have the option of dropping either a style or a dying brand OR to re-invent their line which is known as a "PLC re-curve." Consumer packaged goods companies will do this via a "new and improved" strategy or they may offer a dramatic improvement in price in an attempt to maintain consumer loyalty. In today's beer market, it is imperative for brewers to take a hard look at a style or SKU that just might not be selling anymore. This is a tough decision as brewers are passionate about their brands and beers. The numbers, however, do not fib. If you don't make that call, then the retailer will. When this happens you risk the trust you have with that retailer and wholesaler. The retailer may even drop your entire line thinking that your brand is losing favor with his/her clientele. With so many new entrants and the craft consumer's fickle nature, it is an easy decision to make, particularly if the retailer has an understanding of category management.

A knee jerk reaction to re curve a brand in the Maturity stage is to discount. This may make sense for some products but if your brand has been built and positioned as a high end product, this temptation can be addicting and life-threatening. I have seen a number of suppliers who know that their brand is plummeting towards the Decline stage. Their strategy to postpone the inevitable is via radical discounting. The problem with this path is that both the supplier and the wholesaler lose money via a much tighter margin. If the retailers extend the discount then they will also reduce their margin. The problem with regular deep discounting is that both the retailer and consumer become trained on price. As a result, they wait to buy your brand and won't touch it when it's at full price. This would be similar to buying men's suits.

A word of caution based on experience, as you continue to discount your beverage, you take it down the commodity road, which is a one-way street. Perhaps your six packs once sold for $9.99. When consumers see them at $5.99 then they will associate the brand's quality with that price point. They will also wait to buy at $5.99 or they will buy from a competitor when your products are not at that new price threshold. When you try to go back to $9.99 or even $8.99, the brand will not sell because it has lost that premium cache in the consumer's (and retailer's) mind set. No marketer can rebuild the equity in a super-premium after it has been discounted with great frequency.

As mentioned, pricing becomes a key manipulation variable once a brand enters the Maturity stage of the product life cycle. One tactic that some beverage companies have used is called a "tactical post off" which is a significant departure from their conventional every other month post off discount. The typical every other month post off is $2.00 per case while a tactical post off, which is usually posted for either ONE day only or a week long, maybe be as deep as $5 to $6 off per case. This deep discount strategy can capture some decent short term volume but only slows the brand's demise slightly. The supplier will soon learn that they need to apply the tactical discount with greater frequency which in turn results in bridge buying. My suggestion to suppliers is not to exceed three tactical post offs per year in order to shield some brand equity.

Another option is what I call a, "hybrid tactical" which is a not quite as deep as a tactical (thus preserving a bit more margin) but more enticing to the retail buyer as the price is deeper than the every other month post off. For example, perhaps you are having a problem with clearing out a slow moving seasonal style and need to make room for the next. A possible strategy would be to offer a hybrid tactical to the retailer which is more attractive than the post off but sold on select SKUs so as to protect the brand franchise from a discounting frequency expectation.

A unique nuance in the Maturity Stage is that this period oftentimes signals the end for that style of beverage that you may be very attached to. These can be difficult decisions to make but must be made in favor of what Kim Jordan, owner of New Belgium Brewing defines as a "vibrant portfolio." Keeping SKUs past their prime is a quick way to lose face with both your retailer and your distributor. A savvy beverage marketing team should always be working with the brew masters (and R&D) on the next couple of hits for the brand. These can be formally tested via focus groups and quantitative marketing research or more simply through tasting rooms and beer festivals. Consumers will quickly indicate preference for winning new beverage and beer styles. As you ponder these "disco" decisions temper them by the DEMANDS of your target market. Today's craft beer drinkers want variety, change and quality; ALL at the same time. That might just be a marketing strategy brewing right there...

Decline Stage – Fourth Gear, The Thrill is Gone

In the Decline stage, sales are clearly headed in a southward direction while distribution is spotty and falling off rapidly. Brands begin to turn up in discount retailers, a channel in which they would have never belonged back in the introduction and growth stages. These low end retailers contribute to the brand's demise as consumers perceive the brand to be lower in quality and freshness. Price point substantiates these perceptions as the brand is available at price points never seen before. When a high end brand begins to appear in these types of retailers, then the time is near for the brand to be buried. Few if any brands have come back from the Decline stage. Once a brand takes this path there is no return from "the commodity highway."

It cannot be over emphasized about how important it is to manage your brands away from the Maturity and Decline stages of the product life cycle. Many brewers are accelerating this process by introducing far too many styles within their product line. In essence, they are over extending or producing far too broad a product line. By doing this, many of the

SKUs will end up in discount retailers as wholesaler and supplier sales teams are unable to sell these marginal SKUs to retailers or On Premise buyers. Once these SKUs land in discount retailers, this action will affect the brand positioning of the ENTIRE brand line. In essence, by dropping your brand into "dollar store" type outlets, you are essentially accelerating the brand's trajectory downward towards the Decline stage. Heed this warning as your brew master tells you that he/she has another new SKU to introduce. Only the strongest brands will survive in the marketplace. Marginal ones should not be introduced, restricted to brewpub selling only or replaced with new and positively tested styles.

III- **B**OSTON CONSULTING MODEL – ANOTHER MEASURE OF BRAND HEALTH

Back in the Seventies a consulting group located in Boston devised the Boston Consulting Group Model which has evolved somewhat over the decades. The thought behind this model was to determine improved methods for managing a portfolio of brands (or companies) to ultimately become more profitable and to generate more cash flow via sales volume.

BOSTON CONSULTING GROUP MODEL

RELATIVE MARKET SHARE

		High	Low
RATE of INDUSTRY GROWTH	High	**STARS**	**PROBLEM CHILD**
	Low	**CASH COW**	**DOG**

The model allows for brands to be categorized into one of four classifications. Each category carries with it significant brand implications with specific strategic options. Once a manager has decided where his/her brand resides, then appropriate strategies can be devised to either maintain that spot in the matrix or to improve brand position moving "up" to another spot within the model. When overlaid with the product life cycle, these two tools or "brand thermometers" become very powerful for the senior beverage manager. Having a clear understanding of your brand(s) and where they objectively reside within this analytical competitive framework will allow for improved decision making and reduce risk in making these decisions. The Boston Consulting Group Model looks like this[15].

This powerful analytical matrix allows the manager to decide where his/her brand fits/resides in the marketplace. As you study the model you can see that the "X axis" pertains to relative market share while the "Y axis" is based on industry growth rate. A brand that competes in an industry with a high rate of growth – such as the craft beer market – is already in a good place. This is one of the primary reasons for the incredible brewery expansion/explosion in the US. The X axis, however, is where the malt hits the road.

Many brands reside in the two, low market share boxes for a variety of reasons. The easiest one to explain is time in the market place. Newer brands will have less market share because they are just entering the Introduction stage of their product lifecycle and have not had the opportunity to capture large chunks of market share as they build distribution, focus on trial/sampling and select wholesale partners. These craft beer brands could therefore be categorized as "Problem Children." That is, they are in an industry with a high rate of growth but currently have low market share. This is a good position to be in, however, as the goal is to move the brand one space over to the "Stars" category.

Brands like Boston Beer, Sierra Nevada, Anchor Steam, Stone Brewing, Lagunitas, and New Belgium Brewing have all made this move. The end goal is to have as many brands in this category as possible. The other side of being a Problem Child is the possibility of sliding south into the "Dog" category which is both low in share and low in industry growth. An extreme example of a product in the "Dog" category might be the typewriter. In the beverage business we might define the wine cooler category as a Dog. Note that the category would also qualify for placement within the Decline stage of the Product Life Cycle. This is typical for a brand or product category that has dropped to "Dog" status.

Managing Your Brand's Future

I have had the pleasure of working with a great variety of brands throughout my career but feel compelled to discuss the consequences of becoming complacent in today's beverage industry, particularly on the craft beer side. There are many beer brands in the US that stagnate in the Cash Cow segment of the Boston Consulting Group Model. This can be an intoxicating place to park your brands as ownership scrubs off brand profits with minimal investment. This ignorance of market dynamics is exactly what will take many fine brands immediately to their commodity doom unless significant action is taken.

To continue to succeed in today's beverage business takes all kinds of talented people including passionate brewers, efficient distributor partners, creative marketing teams and experienced sales managers who know that business does not operate in a vacuum. Remember that hundreds of new brands are coming into the market, many of which will threaten your existing brands for finite Off and On Premise real estate. By sitting back and harvesting profits from your Cash Cow brands, you are quietly investing in their demise. Owners of these brands need to take this advice and invest in "feet on the street", in advertising, in marketing, in relevant styles to their geo-demographic target(s) and in distributor sales team incentive plans to ensure brand vibrancy, pull through and growth.

The Cash Cow position is really not a permanent one, rather it should be temporary as the marketing team prepares a strategy to move up (herd those cattle northward!) into the Star position. If execution is careless, the Cash Cow brand can slide over to the Dog position which is often associated with the Maturity or Decline stages of the product life cycle. Ignoring the impending competitive onslaught will escalate many a once strong brand's demise. You have been warned.

IV- **B**RAND POSITIONING & the "KDA"

As a marketing professional, I firmly believe that to be successful in today's marketplace, you must find a clear differentiating advantage in your brand and in your company personality. Everything that you and your employees do and say about your brand contributes towards the sum perception held by your customers. Look at it as a cumulative investment, one bottle cap at a time.

Each brand should have a clear positioning as defined by the brewer's, vintner's or distiller's marketing team. Positioning examples include brands like Chimay from Belgium which is a super-premium boutique import and seldom (if ever) sold on price. At the other end of the spectrum there are economy brands that sell very well like Keystone or Miller High Life which come in 30-packs. These are typically sold as price fighter/value brands. One of the finest examples of positioning via long term brand equity investment is Mexican import, Corona Extra. This relaxed, beach-party persona represents a textbook strategy on hammering home to the consumer and all audiences, a consistent brand message that is immediately recognizable and appreciated. After all, who does not love the beach and turquoise blue water?

The strategy employed by Corona's marketing team, in effect, provides the brand with, what UC Berkeley marketing professor David A. Aaker describes as, "sustainable competitive advantage"[16]. The two terms may seem a bit confusing but in Corona's case, they have taken their key differentiating advantage (KDA) and through skillful investment over time, matured it into a highly sustainable competitive advantage. Could another brand successfully challenge Corona Extra's beach position? Highly unlikely. On the topic of brand positioning, I suggest that you study the brand Corona and you will quickly be up to speed. Through sustained cumulative investment; Brand Corona now owns/dominates the beach, laid back consumer mindset sought after and dabbled with by many fledgling brands. Owning this niche within the consumer marketplace will be worth billions to the brand.

Your sales rep that calls on your wholesalers, retailers and importers MUST keep these internal customers keenly aware of your brand's position through cumulative repetition. This includes POS (Point of Sale) materials such as case cards, core buff, neons, glassware, shelf or rail strips, floor decals, cooler stickers and metal tackers as well as sales plan incentives or PFPs (Pay for Performance). It is your rep's job to extend "or bridge" this position from your marketing team into the nooks and crannies of the marketplace. This can be done most efficiently through the distributor and their powerful, ubiquitous selling teams. Your rep must also get this message to the consumer level through all available channels such as local media, weekend festivals, community events, etc.

The brand's KDA may not be as transparent as a brand's umbrella or overall positioning. The supplier's (brewer, distiller or vintner) marketing team, however, is challenged to further define and simplify the brand by specifying and exploiting the brand's KDA. The KDA is a product's SINGLE most unique attribute or benefit. Preferably some salient point that no other brand can lay claim to or easily duplicate. The goal is to own this spot within the consumer's black box. This is the place in each consumer's mind where only the most clearly defined brands are tucked away. This is where brand loyalty lives and thrives. The KDA supports the "why I buy that beverage" behind the consumer's loyalty. It contributes to the physical act of reaching to the shelf for your six-pack.

Another beverage that has a clear KDA is Anchor Steam. Their key differentiating advantage is the fact that the brand is, "San Francisco's original steam beer." Corona can also claim to be America's number one import while Coors Light was the official sponsor of the NFL and NASCAR. A more current example is Ommegang Brewing's Game of Thrones ale. This brilliant tie in with one of cable television's hottest medieval series helps to differentiate the brand while associating itself with a mega hit series enjoyed by adults – the majority of which are over twenty-one. It is also something to which no other beverage brand can lay claim. A fictitious KDA for a craft beer would be, "Lake Tahoe Tavern Ale: the only premium beer brewed with pure Lake Tahoe water."

Not to be confused with the brand's positioning statement, the KDA is your brand's most pertinent point of difference *separating or distinguishing* it from the competitive brands, all vying for your space and consumer mind share (that black box). Identifying, crystallizing then investing in this KDA via repetition and promotional exposure will help you win this battle for space as both your internal and external customers begin to remember AND ASK FOR your brand based on the recall and reputation of this KDA. The KDA also differentiates your BRAND from others and prevents it from being perceived as a commodity by your target audience.

This is oftentimes the case with water as trade buyers will conveniently lump "liquids" into this category then authorize shelf space based on price only. This is where you must fight to keep the KDA top of mind with ALL of your publics. Another old-school example of a brilliant KDA is Home Pride bread. Back in the '60's most families consumed white bread led by market leader, *Wonder*. *Wonder* was baked by the Hostess Baking Company; however, in 1965 they decided to introduce a premium loaf – Home Pride, which sold well. The brand really picked up sales with the 1972 introduction of Home Pride Wheat. The KDA for this brand was that it was the only bread that had added butter placed in the top of the bread and allowed to bake into it. This taste/quality advantage propelled the brand to a top three position near market giant, *Wonder*. This is precisely the type of advantage that a beverage marketer should seek and exploit.

It is therefore vital that you go to market with a KDA, which in essence, is your brand's body armor, without it, your brand will be defenseless and be considered irrelevant in the marketplace. Would Iron Man fight bad guys without his protective body suit? By ignoring a discernable point of difference, the consumer and retail (On and Off Premise) buyer will perceive your brand as a replaceable commodity; most likely purchased solely on the basis of price.

When a brand turns down the commodity road, there is no going back as this is a dark, one-way street at the intersection of Decline Stage Alley and Dog Avenue. Thus the reason to hire a marketing team, ad agency or consultant to spend the time up front to uncover and strategically determine the optimum methodology to IDENTIFY and EXPLOIT this unique point of difference. As mentioned earlier, this is much more than telling a story on how the company came to be. The KDA is the lifeblood of your beverage; the DNA that will dictate survival or death by commodity declaration.

HEINZ Ketchup and Opportunity Shelf Cost

Why has Heinz Ketchup been the number one product in the ketchup category since the invention of the tomato? Because they do not over segment the brand. They also maintain logo and quality integrity. These are three key elements of their success and should be noted by the reader. I have seen many beer brands, to my amazement, change their logo from the flagship brand (and even their successful brand name, remember Haywire...?) on product line extension packaging, which only serves to further confuse the consumer. Would Heinz do this? Would they alter their logo if they came out with a Heinz Ketchup with Onion Bits? They would do no such thing as it would negatively influence brand equity. Do the brewers do this intentionally thinking that if the extension is not a success then it won't hurt the brand franchise? Of course it will.

The lesson here is to maintain consistency with your logo, and packaging, develop a solid logo up front that emphasizes the brand's KDA and invest in it, repeatedly (it's called brand equity), so that your consumer knows what it looks like and the great product inside that it represents. This is by nature the definition of branding. We buy the product with the expectation of a quality and need satisfaction level, every time. That is what contributes to brand loyalty and repeat purchase and that is why we all return to Heinz: expectation consistency.

When you think about Heinz Ketchup, what comes to mind? As you ask yourself this, and you look at your potential SKU count which might exceed fifty, for example, ask yourself if the consumer is even going to be able to remember what your brand or brewery is best known for when buying the extension or "seasonal of a seasonal?" The potential danger will be consumer confusion and their departure from your brand to a competitor's. I feel it best to stick with what you do best. Don't overextend into styles or beverages of which you have little knowledge or expertise. Do not introduce new items based on ego, trend or fad.

Example

Let us take a fictitious brand such as Truckee River IPA that has successfully performed well into its Growth stage. The logo of the Truckee River Brewery resonates with the consumer as he/she knows that they will get a high quality IPA every time he/she buys a six pack from the retailer or orders a pint at his/her favorite bar. As a result, Truckee River Brewing makes a name for itself, i.e., via credibility, based on its IPA consistency. They then introduce an amber, wheat, lager and stout under the Truckee River Brewing logo. These extensions make sense as they are natural for the base brand which earned its consumer trust ("cred") with its IPA.

What doesn't make sense is the introduction of four Belgian style ales that really taste alike but serve to confuse the consumer which further distances them from the reason they became loyal to the Truckee River Brewery in the first place. They will then begin to wonder what it was that attracted them to the brand. That is when you can lose your customer base. This lengthy example is not to say that new products should be avoided, it is simply a warning to remain within your brand's comfort/expertise level, just like Heinz Ketchup has over the past centuries. When in doubt, ask yourself, "Would the Heinz brand team do this?"

Zig vs. Zag

Not all brands have clear cut KDAs but a savvy supplier-side marketer or ad/promotional agency partner or experienced consultant should be capable of uncovering your brand's most salient strength and use that to position the brand in the minds of your customer wholesaler and buyer base. It may take some doing but your team MUST scour their brains for a KDA given the onslaught of coming competition. If not, your brand may be seen as an "also ran" by the buyer or distributor partner that you so need to rally behind your brand or by the consumer who has such a variety of beverage choices when visiting his/her favorite retailer or bar. As a reminder, the KDA should be promoted in the field via all options including Off and On Premise Point of Sale materials.

With a greater number of brands comes competitive effort to duplicate or copy leading brands or styles. Aggressive competitors will see opportunity in various beverage categories once dominated by just one or two brands. An example is the Cider business. This category has quietly been growing at a triple digit pace over the past few years. Today the category is expanding to include "craft ciders" like Jillian's, Crispin, Two Rivers and others while Vermont Cider continues to swallow up large existing brands seeing this category as a long term home. The large beer companies are also getting into this category with their own brands. What does this mean to a brand that may not have as large a war chest as these new entrants? Perhaps it is time to "Zig when the others Zag." This strategy, popularized by soft drink companies in the eighties, is currently in play within the craft beer industry.

Many of the smaller brewers are not following consumer trends or their competitive much larger brewers, rather they are creating their own styles with unconventional ingredients. A great example of a brewer doing this is Dogfish Head. Sam Caglione has a passion for creating beers that have been dormant for centuries and bringing them back to life with his company's spin on them. This in essence is the company's KDA. When everyone else is brewing high hopped IPAs, Dogfish head is brewing classic, esoteric styles with their own spin to them.

Another example is Mateveza Brewing in San Francisco who is using Mate instead of hops in their brewing process. The result is an outstanding brew, not available from any other brewer. This zig vs. zag strategy makes it hard for competitors to duplicate or dilute Dogfish Head or Mateveza Brewing SKUs while it also provides clear differentiation to the craft drinker, the sales person and the retail or bar Buyer who all appreciate and understand this strategic and unique point of differentiation.

A further example of Zig vs. Zag is in brand advertising. The larger brands rely on media artillery such as thirty second ads on the super bowl. Smaller brands, particularly crafts, know that television is not the medium for their brands because "big media" also conveys "big brands" in the mind of the viewing audience. Media vehicle selection should effuse from brand positioning, however, savvy brands can "zag" from their competition via guerilla marketing events like art and wine jazz festivals, blues and bar b que car shows and other unique, off-the-beaten-path marketing options which lend to brand discovery, trial and KDA exposure.

"Story Marketing" vs. Conventional Branding

Much has been said and written about the importance of "story telling" as a primary marketing strategy. In my opinion, this is where brewer egos with little, if any marketing experience/expertise arrive at the wrong conclusion. If your brand has a unique story behind it, then yes, this should be considered as "ammo" or a contributing piece to the overall marketing strategy and communications campaign. It should not, however, be viewed as the foundation or marketing platform for the brand. The story behind the brand contributes brand building blocks and should be communicated as a Key Differentiating Advantage. I would also suggest that if the story is unique and adds value to brand equity that a professional copywriter be hired to creatively wordsmith the story so that it can be discovered on a web site, Facebook page, in a tasting room, retail account, etc. Think of this story as the marketing/sales copy that entices your prospective customer to the brand and then convinces or persuades him/her to buy it. The story, if written correctly, will get into the consumer's "black box" where it will reside with other loyally purchased brands known as the evoked set. It should work equally well with potential retail buyers who need to hear this story.

Understand that great marketing is so much more than telling a story. Story telling is important as it engages the consumer enticing him/her to learn more about you and your liquid. But Marketing leverages all the brand's positives and synergistically presents them in their finest combined form to your internal and external audiences. Do not think that there is a short cut to marketing and don't assume expertise where it is not. See the story, as the opening of the front door to your brand. A good one (story) will bring consumers into the entry way where the marketing campaign welcomes them inside for a full view/experience.

V- CROSS POSITIONING – CO-BRANDING – LINKING WITH BRANDS THAT REFLECT UPON YOURS

I happen to have a passion for muscle cars and have been a shade tree mechanic since I was 14. During college breaks I often worked on people's cars and charged them by the case of Heineken. We had some pretty good dorm parties back then. This passion has allowed me entry into trade-only shows such as SEMA (Sports Equipment Manufacturer's Association started by Vic Edelbrock) that is held once a year in Las Vegas, Nevada. If you are a performance "gear-head" then this is THE show for you. Every major performance product manufacturer is in attendance from FORD Racing and Hooker Headers to Ferrari and Good Year Tire Company. It is so huge that it takes a speed-walker three days to get through it.

The beauty about this show is that you get to speak with the engineers and techs that create and build the parts that make extra horsepower, better handling, etc. The SEMA show is one of the two largest shows that comes to 'Vegas each year. It is so huge that it takes up both convention halls in the city, all floors inside such AND the vast parking lots surrounding both convention sites. The parking lots, which span further than a small city, showcase some of the world's hottest and coolest cars. Everything from muscle cars and race cars to futuristic concepts and famous movie vehicles are in attendance. SEMA is THE top show on the planet for cars of this caliber. Having your car in SEMA is the highest level of recognition achievable in this country, if not the world. I will now share my SEMA "marketing" revelation…

As my fiancée and I jumped out of the cab dropping us off at a recent SEMA show I was again amazed at this automotive spectacle. It was overwhelming, but in a very cool way. I moved slowly towards one of the many entrances not wanting to miss anything. We could not help notice the massive tour buses parked to our right. We decided to check this out and went over to see an outdoor party for what seemed to be for 10,000! A vast area of the south parking lot had been roped off for the DUB Wheels "booth." This was a car show within a car show! There must have been over three hundred muscle and assorted classic cars and trucks all featuring DUB's ultra-huge diameter wheels. DUB's team had also hired a DJ, lots of attractive spokes models and set up the center area with dozens of couches, easy chairs and tables for lounging or speaking with DUB sales reps after a long walk inside the convention center.

As a marketing professional, I was intrigued by this significant investment on the part of DUB and fascinated with their strategy. After all, they had most if not all of the major tire and wheel buyers from around the world right there in the parking lot. As I walked into the inner circle, I noticed beverages being served including Corona beer. "Hmmm, I thought, why just the one brand....?" I swung around to my left to get a better look at the Godzillian-sized DUB-branded tour truck caravan spanning over a half-mile. Each of the huge fifty-three foot trucks was wrapped in exquisite branded detail. "Join us for the DUB Wheel Tour...sponsored by....." To my amazement there was a list of over a dozen brands including Monster and Corona that were paying DUB to cross promote their brands via DUB's marketing tour of significant trade shows such as SEMA. Now this is brilliant marketing!

What makes this so incredible is the cross positioning of mega brands like Corona with DUB Wheels. Think about it. Both brands appeal to the same target audience – males over 21 years of age and both benefit from participating together. In essence, a brand synergy is created. Other "less cool" brands were also sponsors. The rather boring brands made this investment to bolster their positioning in the minds of this crucial and difficult to reach target audience. The result is that sleepy or aging brands can prop up their positioning and be seen as "cool" or at least somewhat more relevant by this prized target audience. This osmotic "brand sponging" approach is brilliant even if they are not fully accepted by the target audience. The participating brands still benefit to some degree via their affiliation with DUB and the other cool brands such as Corona and Monster.

Monster's participation was even bigger than in year's past with a full force sampling team handing out complimentary sixteen ounce cans of their new product adjacent to their radical 1969 Camaro display. They also sold scale model versions of the Monster-branded Camaro getting the brand home to the lucky recipient of the model. Monster also sponsored two FORD Mustangs participating in an exciting drifting show that spanned over another third of the expansive parking lot.

On the perimeter of the lot were the additional DUB and Monster energy drink semi-trailers, all custom-painted and waxed up for the SEMA show. You could not take a photo without getting these brands somehow into your view finder which ultimately ended up on someone's Facebook page. The branding strategy, trial, sampling, sales and synergy were epic, all contributing to each participating brand's equity bank. Finally, some of the automotive manufacturers featured 2013 model cars with the DUB wheels in this display bringing more attention to these new models and brand excitement generated by the DUB marketing team.

This lengthy example serves as creative fodder for the craft brewer, the non-alcoholic beverage company, the small-medium spirits distiller and/or the winery that needs to create a solid positioning around their brand. Some of the sponsoring companies did this by way of association or cool, brand sponging. If you are still scratching your head on why I shared this experience with you then just review the demographics and compare them to your beverage lineup. Most likely the audience will index at the highest level for your brand period. The people that attend SEMA are also gatekeepers or influencers of others who enjoy sharing their experiences.

(Photos taken by author)

Many of you reading this book will not yet have the resources to participate in such a grand Zig vs. Zag relationship like the one outlined between DUB, Corona, Monster and FORD Motor Company. The reason for the "heavy ink" on the concept is more to stimulate ideas and recognize local opportunities in your market that will generate trial and gain brand awareness. To that end, I have been experimenting on a much smaller scale, and with excellent results. With 78 million baby boomers residing for the most part in the US, there is a tremendous pool of 'boomers' that have a passion for muscle and classic cars. The Gen X generation, born between 1961-1981 represents another 84 million and also appreciates cool cars like their boomer parents. (Source: Wikipedia).

Both vehicle categories (muscle and classic) continue to rise in value. Take for example, a 1966, 427 Shelby Cobra, which can easily sell north of $1,000,000. This love and passion for cool, performance cars represents an opportunity for savvy beverage marketers. The opportunity lies in the omnipresent spring, summer, fall weekend art-and-craft festivals held in nearly every US city. The organizers of these events are always hungry to increase attendance which results in higher booth occupancy, more and larger sponsors and greater income.

One creative option to work with these producers is through local car clubs. What I've started doing at weekend festivals is to convince the event producers to allocate space for a muscle and classic car show to be held within the fair itself. Owning two Shelby GT-500s, I get feedback on the concept from the trenches. Since I also have special event responsibility with my employer, we negotiate a craft/micro tasting booth adjacent to the car show of about one-hundred cars. The car club members own these cars to share and enjoy them with others who are prospective customers of yours.

These festival opportunities provide the car owners with a great weekend activity in which they essentially are the rock star/celebrities at the event. Keep in mind the car club owner demographic and the gatekeeper status that they possess. They, too, are your customers and LOVE to share their brand experiences with others. Think of them as brand ambassadors in waiting. All you have to do is convert them.

Within the car show section we can sometimes negotiate a craft/beer tasting booth. Without a doubt this booth is the most popular at the entire festival which typically spans multiple city blocks. The producer of the event charges $10, for example, for three tastes of microbrews. The beer is usually donated by the smaller craft brewery that would not be able to afford the full beer sponsorship fee which runs in the thousands of dollars. The donation is typically just four to six cases of beer but the exposure, trial and "discovery factor" are tremendous. On the subject of cross positioning (discussed in the DUB wheel example), I also allow one of the smallest craft brewers that I work with to sponsor my Shelbys which serves as a "cool positioning tool" for the brand via association. This minimalist cost to them has already included a live TV interview and web site photos that include the brand with the two "Shinerunnin' Shelby" GT-500s.

You might consider sponsoring one of the cooler cars (in your local area) and "pay" them with free beer. For the sponsorship, the car owner would agree to hang a branded banner adjacent to his/her car and to wear a branded shirt or hat. I see this concept as one that will grow as demand for the cars AND the discovery of high quality beverages are what the consumer wants and genuinely enjoys. I could see this same concept work for wines and quite possibly spirits. The concept will also help special event producers get more sponsor dollars as well as increased attendance. The goal should be to brand the car show within the overall festival and pre-promote such, giving the prospective festival participant (male and female) an even greater reason to attend. The same concept could apply at motorcycle shows for a microbrew that might be motorcycle-oriented or a product line of beer named after vintage aircraft at an air show where many beverages are served and sold.

Medium-sized beverage companies might also look to actively sponsor the car/craft sampling area within the overall festival as a strategic guerilla investment. To me, this is an excellent spend as it further props a fledgling brand into the cool car limelight instantly garnering such by way of "reflective association." This would be a solid option for an aging brand in the Maturity Stage. Cumulative investment in this "show within a show" concept would be an advisable yearly strategy provided it is a positioning stage that the beverage company owners see as appropriate to their brands. It is, however, an untapped opportunity in a time when most unique marketing platforms are long dominated by mega consumer packaged goods and/or Fortune 500 brands.

The medium-sized brewer, for example, might even look at pouring multiple draft styles in a tap takeover approach. A small to medium sized beverage company, such as a craft beer might share costs with a regional or larger bar-b-que sauce manufacturer and include bar-b-que at the car show along with the craft beer. This would increase consumer interest even more (who doesn't love bar-b-que?) while keeping them in that part of the show for a longer period which equates to more exposure time for your brand and more opportunity to have your rep(s) spread your brand gospel: "Did you know our brand is now available at your favorite retailer?" "Please stop by Shelby's Bar and Grill after the festival for a drink special on our brand…" You just might get some good sound bites which can be caught on video then sent to You Tube and linked through your brand's Facebook and Pinterest pages, as well as the company web site.

As your rep heads to the after event beverage promotion he/she can Twitter their arrival, signaling the beginning of the promotion which he/she sold in the week or two prior to landing that new handle or bottle placement at the non-buy account which now appreciates your community (local) involvement. This is how you dot the "I's" on guerilla marketing tactics. Always keep in mind that retail and On-Premise buyers enjoy attending these art and wine/bar-b-que and blues festivals. I have had multiple sit down conversations whereby the buyer lets his/her hair down to sample a new brand. Inevitably, this leads to an appointment, possibly an authorization. Always be on your toes at these events because you never know who will drop by.

Other Cross Positioning Ideas

Although I do not have a lot of success with the concept that I will detail for you next, I wanted to include this experience as you might get an offshoot idea from it. The concept emanates from the desire to tie a major motion picture to a beverage brand resulting in an even stronger brand positioning within the consumer's mind.

The company I work for is owned by a very large DVD, video game and CD distributor. This parent company is well connected with the entertainment industry and is the nation's largest distributor of DVDs. The movies are sold into the major supermarket and drug chains and all other relevant retailers throughout the channel. My idea was this: tie a craft brand who wants to increase volume sales in a national supermarket retailer to the release of a major motion picture DVD. The idea has been well received by the retailer, the brewer and the studio. The nuts and bolts of the concept include incremental space for the beer as well as the DVDs while the consumer receives an instant four dollars off when he/she purchases both the DVD and twelve-pack of the sponsoring craft beer. Merchandising has been agreed to that incorporates the film, the beer and the DVD release. The creative is to be printed in standard movie-poster sizing.

The beauty of this concept is that the brand team also pays for significant product placement within the movie which is filmed in the brewery's hometown. The film is rated "R" so as to not appear as though the retailer or the brewer is appealing to an underage audience. This cross positioning concept reached the final stages, aka "legal" when it was learned that the star of the film's contract forbade any post alcohol-related promotions associated with the movie(!). That was a dark day for this marketing guy.

Although the concept did not get to execution level, the idea is a decent one and something that could be executed by a larger craft, wine or spirits producer. The DVD tie in with an instant redeemable coupon also might work for a languishing brand that needs some "re-positioning" or for a brand that suffers from low awareness. Either way, the notion of a combined DVD purchase with a quality twelve pack might just be the ammo that you need to convince that mega chain buyer that your brand deserves a chance in his/her chain. As the dog fight for dwindling shelf space escalates, it will take out of the keg ideas like this one to get your brand noticed and in the door.

Yet another idea possibility is Match.com, the largest on-line dating company in the world. Match is finally getting around to seeing the "marketing light" by organizing single/mingle parties across the country. What it entails is members are alerted to or are invited by potential suitors to these evening events that typically take place at, you guessed it, bars. A brewer or tenacious beverage company could exploit this exceptional opportunity by working with the Match.com marketing team and helping with "pre" bar selection.

Take a minute and think about how powerful this concept could be in the hands of your sales rep team. I am referring to the On-Premise animals that are always looking for an extra bullet for their negotiating gun. Even a regional craft brewer could work on sponsoring these parties and helping to set them up in advance at the account. What do you think the buyer would say to your new handle request(s) when you tell them that you plan to bring in over one hundred (maybe quite a few more than that) single drinkers for the evening. If successful, perhaps this party becomes quarterly or even monthly. Accounts love you when you bring them lots of adults who want to drink and eat at their establishments.

The marketing minded brewer might also negotiate with Match.com's marketing team on the inclusion of the brewery logo and brands on the any email announcements, Facebook pages, social media vehicles or that particular spot on the Match.com web site. Maybe your brand sponsors these "mingle parties." Your field reps might take this a step further and sample your brands, where legal to ensure trial. How about a tap takeover or an in-bar (where legal) DVD give-a-way that includes a film with your product in it? This sounds like low hanging hops to me. Match.com's competitors might be interested in duplicating this concept needing a beer, spirits or wine partner, as well as advice on what bars to conduct such events in the major metros across the US. Maybe there is a smart phone app available that allows the potential match suitor to pre buy a drink at his/her favorite bar to entice a prospective date to meet On Premise? You readers with Brew Pubs, how many drinkers do you get through your doors on Tuesday evenings? This co-branding strategy adds a whole new dimension to "Taco Tuesdays." Heck, this could even represent an in for a small craft brewer that is looking to get on base with a key On Premise pub, bar, or nightclub account. What they could do is find out when the next single/mingle party is taking place and go to the account and ask if your brand can be placed on a guest handle for the evening or even a jockey box. You could support with a price feature and some appropriate signage to help promote your brand as well as your potential marketing partner.

Meanwhile your wholesaler could print promotional signage and table tents to support the event. While there, one of your team could announce the event and the rep's arrival via their Twitter account then video tape positive consumer responses to the beer then show this to the account the next week in a recap meeting. They just might take your brand on. Once on, you could then use some of that video and the on premise placement success with select up and down the street accounts as well as with small grocery chain buyers and the brand's Facebook page. This low cost form of guerilla marketing could be just what your brand needs to get a toehold in the marketplace.

Luxury Segment – Let Them Discover While Your Brand Osmotically Benefits Via Association

Another option to invest in brand equity is to sample your brands at events relevant to the brand's positioning as discussed in the previous section. For example, in the US there is a business group called the Luxury Marketing Council. This organization has chapters in major cities across the US. The group conducts monthly or bi-monthly networking events that cater to the financially elite. If your brand plan's primary target is this very difficult to reach consumer ($250,000+ household income) then an organization like the Luxury Marketing Council might be relevant vehicle to sample and expose your products. There most likely will be a sponsorship or participation cost associated with each event but the cross branding benefit and the perceived positioning for your brand could be invaluable.

Keep in mind that most of the attendees at these events are "gatekeepers" or key influencers within their extensive professional and personal networks. If they like you and your brand then word of finger, Facebook "likes," Twitter feed, Pinterest and Linked In comments will go a long way on a fairly shrewd and FOCUSED marketing spend. Through cumulative repetition at these events, you will be able to convert these gatekeepers into loyal consumers AND brand ambassadors. Think of these potential ambassadors as having a minimum gatekeeper influence of over two hundred consumers each. The wealthy certainly enjoy and demand discovering and experiencing the next new thing. They want to be the first to discover (referred to as Early Adopters by marketing research analysts) your brand so that they can tell their contacts about what they have tried.

Think also about food pairing at these upscale affairs to make your dollars go even further by sharing with some of the other participating brands. Perhaps you meet a high end cheese company that wants to share a table with you at the next networking function. As more brands enter the mid-range fray, the high end just might be a place to consider for your brands. In closing, keeping with the concept of brand association, think about the value in offering your brewery as a venue for a future Luxury Marketing Council function. Many of you won't be able to execute this idea, however, I set this up for Anchor Brewing in San Francisco, California. The results were very good for the brand as many of the wealthy, white-collar attendees told me personally that they had never tried Anchor Steam beer OR that they had tried and liked Anchor Steam but had no idea of all the other beer styles offered by the brewery.

The key here is to have the ability to step back from your daily routine and look at what makes your operation different from others and the potential value it represents to the marketing function. Anchor Brewing has one of the most exceptional breweries in the United States so exploiting this asset was a natural while the Luxury Marketing Council fit was logically appropriate for all participants.

Upon studying the demo and psychographics of $250,000+ income earners relating to beverages, I have learned that higher price does in fact equate to perceived higher product quality with this segment and most others for that matter. Although not earth shattering news, this segment will certainly test this theorem to its fullest. If your brand delivers exceptional quality thereby meeting this group's stringent expectations then they in turn will respond with solid brand loyalty which will include social media recommendation. If the brand is front line priced, however, far above its quality level then it will die a quick death with this sophisticated segment.

Imported Belgian beers as well as domestically brewer Belgian style beers have enjoyed impressive growth over the past few years. Equally fascinating are the price points charged and maintained for the beers imported from Belgium as they tend to enjoy inelastic demand. This rare phenomenon usually reserved for such commodities as gasoline/petrol will only remain as long as the quality is maintained. The Belgian-style trend has not gone unnoticed by domestic brewers who have feverishly been expanding their product range to include Belgian style sour beers modified by their brew master's spin on the traditional abbeys. I anticipate more interest in Belgian beers, particularly sours, and commend the exporters for maintaining their impressive price points/margins.

Pricing as a Point of Differentiation

In the beer industry, brands are normally discounted or "posted off" every other month or six times per year. The average post off is somewhere around $2 per case of twenty-four, twelve ounce equivalent bottles or cans. This post off typically spans three to four weeks in duration and is posted by the wholesaler in the market. A dangerous trend that I have noticed over the past four to five years is called the "deep tactical post off" or just "tactical" (briefly described in the Maturity-Product Life Cycle chapter earlier). This pricing strategy is used in a variety of ways. One might simply be to blow out bloated inventory or aging product, while another might be to off-set your competition or gain favor with a retailer. The post off should be, but is not always, passed onto the consumer. Accounts that pocket this extra profit are quickly dropped from these kinds of deal opportunities.

From a sales person's perspective the tactical tool is an intoxicating one with serious implications. I have witnessed several brands rely on these tacticals which dramatically impact wholesaler and supplier/brewer margins. On the consumer end, the ultimate buyer begins to expect your brand at that price. As a result, he or she seldom returns to the brand at full price, opting to wait for the deep discount or to buy another brand.

These deep discount strategies also contradict better quality brand image. These repetitive deep discounts in effect, strip away hard fought for brand equity taking the brand deeper down the commodity highway. Once a brand goes down this path, selling six packs for $4.99 for example, it will be nearly impossible to return to regular price points. Keep this in mind when your sales team begs you for discounts on your brand. Does Ferrari discount? Does San Pellegrino discount? Does Rolex discount? Sometimes it is best to maintain your brand position and sacrifice some volume in favor of long term brand health. This is a subject for some deep thought.

On the low price spectrum, Brand Steinlager has been quite successful by claiming the "economy import" niche in the US market. This economical/value position has served the brand well where it has firm command in the best import value for twelve pack slot.

VI – THE FINAL "P"- SELECTING YOUR DISTRIBUTOR and GETTING THE MOST OUT OF THEM

I have sat in quite a few beverage seminars and when the floor is opened up to the audience, brewers, vintners and distillers immediately ask questions about how to select, manage and work with a wholesaler/distributor. Having been on the supplier side, I can empathize with them and feel their impatience and frustration. After all, there are only so many top tier companies in an industry. Once you get down to the "C" level wholesalers, you might not be overly impressed with their ability to perform.

Typically craft brewer evolution begins with self distribution. I have often marveled at the stories shared about luminaries such as Fritz Maytag who used to deliver kegs to the East Bay (Northern California) from his brewery in San Francisco (this is a suburban area that requires traversing the Bay Bridge and the Caldecott Tunnel) and others like Ken Grossman with Sierra Nevada, Michael Funk with Mt. People's Warehouse in Auburn, California and Michael Crete and Keith Bewley with California Cooler. Crete and Bewley, just like Michael Funk, self distributed their brands by loading up their station wagons then selling to "mom and pops" up and down the streets of Santa Cruz, California. These stories, all equally remarkable, lend unique character and consumer fascination points to the brand, and should be cherished, recorded and promoted by your marketing team.

Self-distribution is initially the only option to the small beverage entrepreneur and must be a royal pain. It is, however, important groundwork as key accounts become valued customers and the life blood of the franchise. These key accounts are most likely called on by your target distributor. Developing relationships with these accounts will serve you well when it is time to discuss handing over these chores to your wholesaler partners. As your company grows, you will become large enough to garner attention from local distributors. Once you have a solid base of accounts, it will be time to meet with one, two or three distributors in your preferred geography.

The Distributor Interview

The initial meetings between supplier and distributor are often a light hearted dance as each party tries to feel the other out. Some suppliers are well prepared for these meetings while others tend to make it up as they go. I suggest going in prepared by doing your homework on the distributor. A simple list of questions that I have heard over the years follows:

1-What territory does the distributorship cover?
2-How many days a week does the company deliver?
3-Is there an account or stop minimum – if so, how much is this?
4-Do you have a brand management model in place? If not, who would be our contact person? How are the brand managers compensated?
5-How are the sales teams compensated?
6-Is the sales department set up via channel selling? If not, how so?
7-Who are the senior managers of the company?
8-Will you pick up at our brewery?
9-What are your payment terms?
10-How does your team control freshness and quality codes?
11-How many On Premise and Off Premise accounts does your Company deliver to?
12-Do you deliver to chains such as Whole Foods, Mollie Stone's and other natural/organic chains?
13-Are there any chains that you do not deliver to?
14-What other brands are you looking to add to your portfolio?
15-What is your expected margin on selling draft vs. case beer?
16-Does your team merchandise the shelves?
17-Do you co-op sales plan incentives?
18-What is your sample and donations policy?
19-Do you participate in weekend special events? If so, what are the criteria for brand selection?
20-What is the policy or criteria for wrapping or branding delivery trucks or vans?
21-Does the company have a large cooler for kegs and/or cases for cold storage? If so, what is the average temperature of that cooler?
22-Does the company have a graphics department to accommodate Point of Sale and special event banner requests? If so, is there a charge associated with this use?
23-What is the procedure for picking up old beer?
24-How frequently are empty kegs returned to the brewery?
25-What are the loading dock days and hours? Sample pick up policy?
26-Does the company conduct quarterly or trimester business reviews?
27-What else do you look for in a supplier?
28-Should we decide to mutually end the relationship, what is the method for buy out? Notification requirement? Do you have a standardized contract to review?
29-Does your company co-op chain ad investments?
30-Does your company co-op deep price discounts when needed? (these are sometimes referred to a tactical post offs)

31-Would the senior management team be interested in an equity stake? (if available of course)

32-Does the company allow rep ride withs and crew drives? Get details.

33-Does the distributor have a specialized Craft or Import Division? If so, who manages this?

34-Does the company have a Social Media strategy for the brands?

35-Although not a deal breaker, ask your wholesaler if they conduct beer style seminars for accounts or if they conduct tasting trade shows that target On and Off Premise accounts. If they do, you, the smaller brewer, might get a rare one on one opportunity to sell a significant account directly.

36-Does the wholesaler's sales team call on the Convenience store channel? If so, with what brands? This is a key question since the two multi-national factory brewers control the shelf captain role at all of the major US convenience store chains which results in craft and import brand exclusion. If you learn that your prospective wholesaler has very limited success in the C-stores then you will want to deploy limited resources elsewhere such as the indies or On Premise. If, however, your distributor is able to gain shelf access to their convenience stores via franchising groups that stray from corporate plan-o-grams, then you might even consider samplings (where legal) because according to Craft Business Daily (11/30/12) the core craft and casual craft beer consumer account for 88% of c-store craft consumption. So if you can't do some tastings then be sure to get point of sale in the stores to steer and educate them towards your brands.

37-In an average week, how many new handles can your On Premise team procure? If this figure is under three then you might want to reconsider appointing this distributor.

38-Can your distributorship execute tap take overs at large On Premise accounts?

39-Are any of your staff Cicerone or Sommelier certified?

40-Can your warehouse accommodate your brand temperature/storage requirements?

41- Would you financially contribute to a sales rep in the area either on a co-op or cents per case basis?

42-Does the wholesaler have a category management team?

Over the years it has amazed me to watch how various brewers treat the distributor relationship. Many feel that their "selling job" is complete once they have secured that long sought after contract. These suppliers do not understand how the system works because they have either never worked for a wholesaler or have conveniently classified them as a commodity element within their business model. Do not forget the sagely advice given to you earlier. These suppliers are the type that rely completely on the distributor to sell the brand, set up and execute special events, generate sales plan (Pay for Performance) incentives and brand merchandising. Thinking that you are in the Red Zone after you have appointed your distributor simply means that you will slide to the lower end of the distributor team's focus. The next tough phase begins, that is, selling to the distributor team – from receptionist to president and all in between.

Once your distribution footprint is in place, the next most important step that you MUST take is to hire feet on the street. That is, you MUST hire tenacious field reps to sell your products and work with your wholesaler sales people in the Off and On Premise accounts. Not having a field rep on your team, or at least planning to hire one, will most likely result in the wholesaler's rejection of your brand. This point cannot be over emphasized nor can it be under estimated by any beverage supplier – alcoholic or non.

VII- **D**ISTRIBUTOR DYNAMICS – Just What Makes These Guys Tick?

Now that you have inked all contracts with your distributors, where do you go next? As mentioned, some brewers/suppliers think it's time to smoke a cigar and look to the next distributor. This is a foolish mistake as the distributor manager who senses this will simply put your brand at the bottom of the pallet. The next step is to commit human resources to the marketplace. The best way forward is to appoint a local rep or two or even three to work the market with the distributor sales teams which sell into the On Premise (night club, bars, restaurants, hotel/motel, taverns, delis, etc.), the Chains (supermarkets, drug, wholesale clubs, etc.) and the Off Premise (up and down the street/mom & pop liquor stores, convenience stores, etc.).

Riding with the distributor sales teams is imperative for a brewer, particularly a smaller one with fewer financial resources to invest in sales team incentives. It goes back to my grandfather's preachings on human nature: people will buy AND SELL for those that they like. Only you can instill and share your passion into the distributor sales person. Your first goal should be to educate the sales person (with the ultimate goal being the entire team) on your key brand elements so that each sales person that your employee "touches" becomes an ambassador for your brand.

Your second goal should be to get in front of your "internal customer" as frequently as possible. Most distributors hold weekly sales meetings which suppliers can often present. This incredible opportunity to crystallize positive opinion for your brand is often times squandered by suppliers/brewers for a variety of reasons. I have sat through decades of "presentations" whereby the supplier/brewer sales rep or managers were completely unprepared to present to this most crucial customer in their sales model. Perhaps it harkens back to the way suppliers perceive distributors or it might just be laziness mixed with big egos. The fact is, few suppliers/brewers take the time to deliver a professionally prepared and rehearsed presentation. This is picked up on within the first sixty seconds by the street smart sales person sitting in the audience. If a supplier/brewer rambles on wasting the sales person's time, they will tune out the presentation in less than a minute. I can't tell you how many times I've seen this happen.

Preparation opens the door for the brewer/supplier that does his/her homework and sees presentation as a way to break through the competitive clutter. Do not take this crucial artillery for granted – respect, invest and educate it.

Communication – Involve the Troops – Get Them to Like YOU More Than Your In-House Competition

On the topic of route salespeople and how suppliers or management may take them for granted or perceive them as low on the priority hierarchy, I recall my experience working in management for a large bread company. I was brought in specifically to fix their problems with the nation's largest retailer and to reverse rapidly declining market share. After a few months of researching and identifying key issues, I realized there was a cavernous gap between the sales/distribution arm of the company and senior management. You see, the sales force grew tired of constantly being dictated to by the big bosses in their ivory tower offices and never being told of what was happening or was about to happen.

Part of my strategy, as a mid-level manager, was to try to reduce this gap via communication. The first step was to develop a motivating Power Point presentation that touched on big picture IRI successes with the chains and then filtered down to individual route accomplishments by salesmen. I closed with an informational company update including new products, packaging, etc. I also included a brief survey asking for the sales reps' opinions on what products they thought the company should bake/sell?

Since bread sales people begin their routes at 4:30 am, I realized that the effort would be useless via print handouts. So I decided to rehearse a road show and met each sales team at their individual bakery/distribution outlet where they loaded their bread trucks every morning. The presentation, sprinkled with some humor, which included weekly updates from made up characters including "Lord Hanky and Captain Doug head" - exceeded my expectations.

These fictional characters became so popular that my memos from them were posted for all to see in the route salesman lounges. This helped to create a buzz and get focus on the troubled chain. The union salesmen (and a few ladies) came up after the presentations often thanking me for sharing the information with them. I lost count as to how many of those hard working guys told me that NO ONE from management had ever done that before or even shared such information with them. This common sense, humanizing effort along with the balance of my restructuring strategy helped to reverse the company's declining market share and to help double it in just 18 months. I can't take full credit here, but the point is that when you can touch such an important gatekeeper on your brand that you do so in such a way as to influence and convert them into your brand ambassadors. If you don't, you still might win the battle because you have great financial resources to back you, but if you don't have the resources and ignore the distributor's sales teams then you will undoubtedly fail.

On the beverage side, we receive superstars occasionally at our distributorship that might be there for a convention, to launch a new product or to assess brand success in one of the Country's major markets. I recall that Boston Beer's founder, Mr. Jim Koch came into San Francisco to make a presentation and then spend a day in the market to see how we were executing on his brand. As I sat at my desk, I again tried to "out creatify" my internal competition. Here I had one of the industry's biggest rock stars coming into the office, but what could I do to exploit this visit?

I made a request to Mr. Koch's PR person for a 5-10 minute interview at the hotel where he was the featured speaker. I submitted my questions that I would ask and got permission to video tape his responses after his presentation. In my interview I included the top five or six salesmen's names based on their Boston Beer performance over the past 12 months. This portion was scripted with a que card but came out great as Mr. Koch congratulated our guys, by name for their specific accomplishments. I used my own digital camera, made some quick edits then showed it in a Friday sales meeting. The entire team was mesmerized by the interview which capped off with Mr. Koch's commending the great work of five to six guys that were sitting in the meeting that morning. They loved it! This is a just a sample of what can be done with some creative thought to include the troops. By including them and recognizing their efforts amongst their peers you will be well on your way to convincing them to be your brand ambassadors.

VIII- CONVERTING THE TROOPS - Winning-Over the Sales Force

One of the best examples I have of a small supplier winning over one of the largest and most powerful distributor sales forces in the US is my experience with Honest Tea. Honest Tea was a tiny non alcoholic company started in Maryland by a student and his professor. Their goal was to provide an organic, healthy RTD (Ready to Drink) single serve tea without mountains of added sugar – just a slight degree of sweetness which also reduced the total calorie count. The product was quite successful but the distribution battle in major markets was extremely challenging. When the small but scrappy Honest Tea sales team came out to San Francisco, they were up against some formidable brands all vying for scarce retail shelf space. The strategy that the Honest Tea team adopted was one of perseverance and roll-up-the-sleeves hard work. The company dedicated two reps to our marketplace. These reps worked ten to twelve-hour-days either riding with our sales team ("ride-withs" are a must for sales team rapport building) or making personal account calls. They also reset shelves, placed merchandising POS (Point of Sale materials) and took care of account deals.

Realizing that they were competing for the attention of these sales people with goliath brewers, wineries and non-alcoholic companies, they increased their efforts by coming to the distributorship at the end of a long day to hand out cold samples of their product to each and every sales person that returned to the office. This gesture was greatly appreciated by the sales force. The Honest Tea guys also dropped cold samples to the President, the two Vice Presidents, the admin team, Tele Sales and the receptionist. They quickly made <u>friends</u> with all the people in the distribution equation.

Taking their efforts even further, they worked with their distributor marketing manager on monthly sales incentives that were "creatively quirky." The incentives were similar to those I created while working for Earthgrains (now Sara Lee) – simple, memorable, profitable (they put dollars into sales people's wallets) and FUN. So many suppliers forget this element in their incentive preparation. We'll get into this topic in detail later in the book. The Honest Tea regional manager also shared my opinion on the value of rehearsed, spirited and creative presentations made to the sales teams which were scheduled every Friday morning, fifty weeks a year.

The Honest Tea guys would come in with cold product for everyone and spend just five to eight minutes in the meeting giving the team a quick update on distribution or volume progress, good news learned during the week which stroked peer egos, new product announcements and most importantly, some cash for outstanding performers. This upbeat, high energy, "hit 'em hard and hit 'em fast" approach was looked forward to by the sales teams and greatly appreciated. This appreciation resulted in extra effort on this small brand which has grown to a national brand recently bought by Coca Cola.

The Weekly Sales Meeting

Most distributors hold a weekly sales meeting, most likely fifty-plus weeks per year. The purpose of these meetings is to gather the team to discuss important brand goals, methods for achieving such, upcoming programs, new hires, new brand lines and communicate internal company updates. Few suppliers/brewers seem to understand the importance of this "internal customer" of theirs. And herein lies the opportunity for you. In essence, it is a chink in the competitive armor. The vast majority of presenters are unprepared, unrehearsed and generally disorganized. As mentioned previously, a street smart team of hardened sales guys/gals will tune out a supplier almost immediately if he/she comes unprepared. The Honest Tea team was one of just a few that were prepared, enthused, upbeat, creative and fun. Several small brewers also present this way and with exceptional results.

A key point to understand is that you will not beat your competition even if you are the best sales person on the planet. Why? Because there is only one of you. To achieve great brand results, you will need to sell/influence as many other sales people on your team as possible. This means transforming the distributor sales force into your brand ambassadors. This task is accomplished cumulatively by repetitive ride withs and sales meeting presentations. Does this mean that you will win the battle by simply showing up every Friday for the sales meeting? No. You must also have something important and relevant to communicate to the sales team in a professional manner. If you come into a meeting and ramble on then you will fall to the rear of the salesman's mindset and gradually diminish your degree of brand ambassador equity invested in each "customer." Think of every presentation you make as brand equity chip investments. A poor performance will take chips away from the equity bucket while a good one will add chips. Lastly, on the subject of the Friday sales meeting, sales people love quality coffee and bagels or Danish. You would not believe the applause that you will get when you make sure that you take care of these people. It's often the little things that yield big results.

Winning Over Distributor Management

Once you have the sales teams humming on eight cylinders there is an equally important group that you will need in your corner. That is senior management. Meeting with senior management on crucial topics shows them your formal commitment to moving the business forward and generates ideas on how to achieve such. Moreover, it strengthens the partnership between you and the distributor as they prepare to allocate resources amongst brands. Many small to middle-sized suppliers don't make this effort. Ignoring this vital step may be the deciding factor to disco your brand entirely. Understand and appreciate that your wholesaler senior managers wield and divvy up substantial assets towards the brands they carry. They also influence your internal customer, perhaps the most valuable team to win over, that being the wholesalers' on and off premise sales forces.

To get the most out of the distributor/wholesaler relationship an annual plan including distribution and volume goals should be shared and discussed a month or two prior to the close of the calendar year. This information can be included in your marketing plan or if you don't have one then you should at least have an annual brand overview or "marketing brief" that details these important points: sales and distribution goals, new product/package introductions, special event participation, key incentive periods, potential price increases, brand KDA, On Premise and Off Premise strategies, significant themes such as July 4th or Cinco de Mayo which may require incremental display requests, as well as, crew drives.

In the appendix is an example of a tool I devised that reviews the prior year's learning's called the Brand Overview. This tool is typically a collaboration between supplier and distributor brand management. The future look or next calendar year document is covered in the Annual Marketing Brief, also located in the Appendix.

Distributors are constantly upgrading their systems and becoming more sophisticated which takes up more of senior management's available "face time." Despite these distractions, you must plan on spending time with them. They may push back if you are a tiny brand but be persistent and they will see and respect you. Most distributors have a knee jerk push back to adding more meetings but will usually soften to the request if it is sincere and good for the business. But be prepared, do not waste their time and have an agenda. I've been in plenty of meetings whereby someone will say, "We never even see those guys. Plus they have no plan around their brand." This is the first step in the "D" listing process.

Even with goliath brands, the adage, "out of sight, out of mind," holds true. There is a fine line between communicating and visiting with your distributor. You can, however, overdo it whereby you become an annoyance to avoid like "beer with floaties" or you can be the supplier that is never heard from or seen throughout the year. If you fall into the latter category, you will most likely be placed at the bottom of the barrel. One distributor senior manager knew that it was January because that was the only time he ever saw his supplier. The old adage, "the squeaky wheel gets the grease," holds true simply by the law of human nature. There is no corollary on distributor management meeting frequency.

You'll learn how often you should meet with these key players as you get to know them, their business, the market and how your brands help the wholesaler grow.

Now that you have a quality distribution model in place and a targeted account list, the real work begins. Your next step must be to bring "feet on the streets" by hiring a quality sales rep on your team. This person will be your direct liaison with the distributor and work closely with the wholesaler and their internal contact, often times referred to as the brand manager. Many distributors are installing craft-savvy brand managers who are the "go to contact" for all your wholesaler needs. This is a brilliant concept born of efficiency which you will quickly appreciate. The brand manager can assist the supplier with all their needs from completing the marketing brief to writing incentive plans or "PFPs" (Pay for Performance) that will generate the placements that your fledgling brand so desperately needs. They can also get sampling cases, handle bill backs, enter new products and generally cut through any red tape that may impede the supplier brand's progress. These are the people that you want to take care of.

If your rep has a bad relationship with your distributor brand manager then get it corrected quickly or get someone else. These relationships are vital as the brand manager can influence your "internal" customer, hat being the distributor sales force. Having a brand ambassador who appreciates your product with passion will result in both short and long term benefits. Bring this person to your brewery so that he/she can meet and drink with your people. Soak them in the brand. Treat them as an "osmotic sponge." A funny thing about this industry is that there is a "Beer Guy code." You earn "code credits" over a period of time with the "beer cowboys" who are the wholesaler/distributor sales team. Once you're accepted, you are described in meetings and presentations as, "a good guy." This moniker goes a long way and is how you want to be characterized when your brand manager presents on your behalf in those weekly Friday meetings. This is an important nuance for someone new to the business to recognize and appreciate.

Brand managers will usually meet with their local or regional supplier reps once per month. Smaller suppliers may only be able to meet once per quarter but this should be the limit. It is important to get that face time for reasons already listed. Each meeting should have an agenda, the author of which typically dictates the meeting. A critical agenda item includes the sales plan incentive, oftentimes referred to as Pay for Performance or PFP. If a supplier has no annual plan then creating a sales incentive is like trying to score a touchdown blindfolded. The marketing brief provides the backbone for the monthly objectives that contribute to the annual strategy. Further, a sharp brand manager can secure prior months and/or historic data on your brand for in-depth analytical review. My advice is to task your brand manager to prepare a monthly scorecard in advance of your meetings consisting of brand case or unit sales by market type. Examples of the scorecard and marketing brief are located in the appendix.

The scorecard is based on internal distributor data and should include key market types such as Bars, Restaurants, Drug Stores, Warehouse Clubs, Supermarkets, Liquor Stores and Hotel/Motels. This tool should also include the percentage up or down AND the percentage of business that each represents to your brand total. This crucial column will indicate where time should be best spent and resources deployed. THIS IS HOW YOU WIN IN THE BEVERAGE MARKETPLACE – do not allow convenience to dictate what you do, analyze the history and see where your brand has weaknesses, your competition has strengths and where to best deploy limited resources to make for maximum efficiency. You would be surprised by how many suppliers ignore the signs and stick to pre-made "mother ship" plans crafted months prior from their headquarter ivory towers. This practice is also how the micro/craft upstart/underdog finds the chink in the armor to exploit with full force.

You might also request that the scorecard include internal data from suppliers with beverages similar to yours, such as crafts/micros. Brands don't need to be identified but the "other" supplier totals (less your brand) will serve as an excellent benchmark for you and your brand manager to manage against. For example, let's say that the "micro cluster" ended 2015 up 12% in the Bars/Taverns segment while your brand was down 3%. That represents a swing of 15 points. Let's also assume that the micro cluster garners 30% of their volume from that segment yet yours garners just 21%. These two red flags indicate an immediate need. That is to get your rep, the brand manager and the distributor sales people selling your brand, into the On Premise, specifically in the Bars/Taverns within that market.

The other need is to write a sales plan incentive to motivate the sales team to perform within that segment. The brand manager can provide a "drill down" report which is a list of all the accounts that comprise the segment. By reviewing this list, you and your brand manager can quickly identify where you have either lost distribution or volume AND where the competing suppliers are having success. This in essence acts as an "attack list" for the next month or two.

As you can see, the scorecard is an excellent tool to take the pulse of your brand. It quickly shows your strengths and weaknesses. It is up to you and your brand manager to interpret this data and generate immediate strategies to "right the ship." Once you have used this tool over a period of time, you will quickly see improvements to each segment. Over a six to twelve month period, the brand's health can be improved dramatically. To effect significant change, however, will require the help of the distributor sales force who typically need something ($) to make their motors run. This investment may be challenging for the smaller supplier but is something they should try to enact for best results. "Thank you's" don't pay the rent nor does a t-shirt.

With the addition of new reps, or feet on the street, should come training that will result in more efficient on and off premise account calls. Be sure that your best sales executive spends time with these reps. I use the following to provide guideline mentoring when my brand team rides with wholesaler sales people. Many of these suggestions are relevant to new supplier/brewer hires.

1-Challenge the new sales rep to create a short objective list prior to entering an account. Go over this list with him/her prior to entering. Train him/her to think this way.

2-As you go through the account, watch closely to ensure that the objective(s) are addressed. After the visit, review the pluses and minuses on how they fared in achieving the objectives.

3-Monitor how the sales rep approaches the customer. Does he/she ask questions? Does he/she probe for needs? Does he/she find out what interests the buyer has such as hobbies, sports or travel? All this data is critical to getting the sale. Teach the rep how to spot clues simply from walking into the account.

4-Study how the sales rep overcomes objections.

> Here's an example: "Bill's Bar." Bill is a bear and oftentimes won't see reps. On my first trip to this account I was left waiting at the bar for Bill for some time. I noticed a turbo charger on the wall and then more car photos of Bill. Finally he came out to tell me that he was too busy that day. Rather than give up, I struck up a car conversation with him. From that point on I got a new Sam Adams handle and booked a Wednesday promo for Sam for the quarter. I did the same thing with the buyer at the old Liquor Barn who scorned sales people.

He would not return my calls until I found out, through his secretary, that he was an avid Raiders fan. She later patched me through so I immediately asked what he thought about the weekend game. I got an hour appointment (that went very long) and was able to book more appointments any time I needed them. Pay attention to detail, find the buyer's buttons, all are different. Remember that people buy from people they like. Teach the reps these skills and the importance of rapport building.

ON PREMISE

5-Teach the rep a methodology or system for success. This includes the importance of booking On Premise appointments, following up on next steps, and taking post meeting notes to record key follow ups.

6-Show your rep how to look at draft handle line ups, styles, ratio of style, brands, competitive bias, and style overload.

7-Observe the bottle line up. What stands out? How does your brand compare to the competition's? Are the brands rotated? Does the account sell cans, if so, what brands? If not, have the rep sell some in.

8-Does the account allow promo/feature POS? If so, are your brands represented? How are the brands promoted – by price or? Does the account allow tap take overs? Food pairings? Is this a foodie account? Could one of your beers be paired with something on the menu? Wait staff trainings? Bucket specials? Pint give-a-ways? Would this be a good account for a future pub crawl? Answers to these questions will help give the rep selling platforms.

9-What stands out in the account as you walk in? Do you see neons, banners, nothing? What type of clientele frequent the account? Does the account have big screens? Do they subscribe to pro sports schedules? This will dictate what to sell there.

10-What Non Alcoholic (NA) beverages does the account sell? What types of food are served?

11-How does the rep handle "black hat" (i.e., pay-to-play) objections? These can be the most difficult to overcome. Some suppliers will participate yet many won't. A possible response to the objection would be to think about what nearby special events your company sponsors. Ask the buyer if he/she appreciates community support for local non-profits. Ask him/her if his/her competitors support the local community. Teach the rep to think about tools that competitors don't have.

12-Did the rep bring cold samples? Stress the importance of cold sampling something new and the opportunity this represents. Everybody likes to see what's new and to try great, cold beer. Cold sampling can be true showmanship if done correctly. Show the rep how he/she can make the buyer feel like a celebrity as others in the bar will wonder who this person is to garner so much attention around great beer.

13-Are there any events taking place nearby that might generate consumer traffic which in turn could be captured by the account and with the help of a branded feature?

14-Talk to the rep about bar personnel evolution, that is, how a bar-back becomes a bartender who then becomes the beverage buyer. Impress upon him/her the significance of the bartender, that of gatekeeper and influencer of brands and sales rep success.

OFF PREMISE

15-After greeting the buyer/owner, ask if you can go to the cooler. Once there, analyze the account's Point-of-Sale (POS). Is your brand dominant? Current? Thematic? How do your neons look? Are they strategically placed?

16-Are the coolers organized in any certain way? Do they need to be reset? Use this service as a selling tool if your wholesaler offers such. Are your brands together in a billboard look or are they grouped by beer style? What is the buyer's attitude about real estate and shelf setting?

17-Is pricing easily noticeable? If not, point this out and get it corrected.

18-Is the beer fresh? Check codes and be sure the rep rotates.

19-Who is the clientele? Is the rep selling to the demographic?

20-Is there any display space? If so, who has it? Is there space near the register that could be used for beer? What is near the register? Are there candy, baked goods, stale fruit or chip displays? Feel the products for dust. If dusty, show the buyer and ask for that real estate for your hot selling beer. This can only happen if you scrutinize the account – and ask.

21-If a high volume account, might this be a buyer to invite to a future baseball or football game or concert to thank them for the business or perhaps to gain additional distribution?

22-What is the condition of the floor? Would a floor decal improve the look while helping to merchandise your brands? These also serve as something of a protector of shelf real estate when they are placed in front of their corresponding brands.

23-In terms of shelf position, how do your brands look relative to eye height and door handle placement? Emphasize the importance of this to the rep.

Another key to successful market entry after appointing your distributor will be via targeted account distribution. That is, pre determine a list of accounts relevant to your brand then tenaciously go to every single one, determined to gain placement. Keep this geography very tight and manageable. It might be as small as several city blocks. The temptation to cover a large area will be defeatist. The best strategy I have seen is when a major city is divided up amongst its relevant neighborhoods. Reps (wholesaler and brewer/supplier) then descend upon each selected neighborhood, striking off each and every account that they win over. Once satisfied, they go to the next and the next neighborhood. At the end of a month's good work they can end up with over one hundred solid and relevant "up and down the street" accounts. The results from these stores can then be taken to the supermarkets during future buyer presentations.

Savvy small company brewers and distillers will need to decide whether or not the big supermarket battle is one that they want to participate/compete in. It may become too expensive to compete for this channel as the multi-national factory brewers continue their blocking strategy against the smaller upstarts. That's not to say that good business is not to be had in the On Premise and up and down the street trade, aka "Indies."

Planting the Seeds

Once you have fleshed out your distribution landscape the next step is to plant the brand seeds in the right places. Despite the desire to generate case volume, the first step MUST be to achieve strategic placement in the marketplace. It is particularly critical that you understand this point and that you begin with a **geographic focus**. Don't make the assumption that you can take the entire United States in one fell swoop. Realize that the US is divided into seven or eight different regions with differing taste preferences as well as psycho-demographic and regional biases. Your brand and sales management teams will need to predetermine if the brand launch will be prioritized through either the On or Off Premise channel. This decision relates to the brand and how it is *discovered* by the target audience. Once this is decided, the distribution focus/effort will be dictated by the type of product or category the brand will compete in.

If, for example, you represent an expensive oak-aged custom barrel scotch whisky from the Isla region, then selective distribution should be your distribution objective. This means that each On and Off Premise account will be reviewed for brand relevance then targeted for placement. A broad-market domestic product, like an energy drink, may therefore be a candidate for every Off Premise account that sells drinks. The point here is to work towards building a brand-relevant, distribution account base through which you can launch either high volume or selective distribution programming as well as communicating your marketing elements. This focused "chess game" approach will serve you well. It will also lend credibility to your brand positioning by representing what your brand team wanted to convey early on in those brand planning meetings typically held a year in advance of the roll out. Try to *match the account* to the brand. Thirty-year single malt whisky will not sell in a dollar store but it will at a five star restaurant & bar or at an upscale, boutique specialty beverage retailer.

Marketing Corollary #3: *Your distribution channel MUST reflect the brand's positioning.*

Making certain that these are in sync is your marketing team's job. The marketing team is the primary protector of your brand and retail selection within the introduction and growth stages should be carefully scrutinized as it relates to the brand's positioning.

Once you have achieved the distribution level that you and your wholesaler have agreed to, you can then look at building volume. When deciding how to motivate sales teams to volume goals, take a look at what other suppliers/competitors are doing. When your team is on ride-withs (a day in the field whereby the supplier representative physically rides with the distributor sales person) have them ask the wholesaler sales person what motivates him/her. He/she will typically respond with "dollars or cash," but do some probing here and you will find other means or ideas that motivate people to new heights and sharper brand focus. One of the worst things that you can do is set a goal so high that no one earns anything on your incentive. This is the quickest way to kill your brand as sales people talk all the time.

There is no clear cut method or formula to determine a sales goal, however, an analysis of distribution (current, past and trending), prior year sales for the period (if available via your distributor's sales data), sales days in the targeted incentive period, competitor sales during the period such as other House craft or import brands and tools such as crew drives, post offs, BOGOs (buy one get one non-alcoholic product deals), weather, etc. are all variables that can impact sales volume. I have learned that an incentive, be it volume or distribution oriented, loses focus if it exceeds two months in duration. Suppliers that insist on three to six month incentives seldom maintain momentum or focus on these extended programs. Keep in mind your internal customer is typically a twenty-something male who wants instant gratification. Do not be tempted to execute what works best for you, rather solicit input from the wholesaler trenches and develop a unique program that will pique their interest while separating your brand from the pack.

X - **C**LUTTER BUSTING INCENTIVES – Creating Incentive Sales Plans That Are Fun, Deliver Results, Motivate, Educate, Tell Your Story, Reinforce Your KDA and Make Money

I recall the results our sales team achieved when they were told that $10,000 cash was on the table and the time that a sales guy won a brand new Dodge Hemi Charger. Most suppliers cannot afford this level of incentive, but they can compete with the goliath suppliers through tenacious creativity. Most large suppliers do not take the time to develop a motivating and unique incentive that also serves as an extension of the marketing plan. The reason for such is due to the fact that regional sales managers are the ones writing these incentive plans not marketing personnel. But this is where smaller brands can find that chink in the armor or "out-creatify" the big companies.

So many suppliers think that $5 per placement or a weekend to 'Vegas or 'Jersey will generate outstanding results therefore earning the supplier managers their bonuses. These retread incentive carrots have been so overused that I saw one supplier add a bag of chips to the $5 pay out as a humorous spin on the overdone $5. As mentioned, this is where the smaller supplier can "get guerilla." This is where you want to spend as much time as you can, with the most creative people you have, or can hire to develop a unique incentive that will bust through the dozens that are put out in front of your internal audience every month. This part is not so easy.

You begin by analyzing what key attributes your brand and company might have over your competitors within your wholesaler's portfolio. If your product is basically a "me too" then you might have to look at $5 and a company sweatshirt. Most brands, however, have a point of uniqueness to them…or something that a creative person can "embellish upon." Case in point: I worked with a small-medium brewer who had a very limited budget and no marketing personnel. The brand was steeped in history as one of the first to enter the craft business in the '80's. They had been passed by, however, due to a lack of brand investment and a sales team that was not particularly motivated. They finally hired a sales rep that was eager to jumpstart the brand and vie for the attention from his internal audience. He did not have a wallet full of dollars but gave me the creative license to "guerilla embellish."

Appreciating the hard job that distributor sales reps have each day, I used a lesson learned back at Earthgrains: taking sales reps away from some of the routine drudgery can lead to incredible results and attention to my brands. So I went out there, "creatively" for a small but long established brewery and fabricated a story about Sasquatch. The lunacy goes something like this: "Sal Squatch" (the "l" was silent) used to work for the brewer but left, never to be seen again. The story had quite a bit more to it while I created a campy video of multiple Sasquatch sightings, interviews, Six Million Dollar Man clips and some other zany pieces. This video was shown in the Friday sales meeting after the larger suppliers had come in with their monotone presentations telling the team what had to be done to win another repetitious trip to 'Vegas or how to earn $5 per placement. The distributor sales force loved the video. The small brand catapulted to top of mind awareness.

I find it easy to generate enthusiasm for underdog brands and positioned the incentive accordingly. The point is to tell a funny or unique **story** that will engage and "hook" the sales team. If they bite, keep it going, that is, internally "brand it" so that the sales force will associate the creativity with your brand. The "Search for Sasquatch" incentive was one of the most successful that the company had ever run. We then followed up with "Sasquatch II" where Sal began stealing kegs from the brewery (this all works because the brewery is in Mendocino County where there have been multiple Bigfoot sightings) and the sales guys/gals earned dollars *and* bags of beef jerky for their efforts.

Over a few more quarters the brand began regaining some of its lost momentum so I decided to take a lesson from Hollywood. About three weeks before the premier of, "Dawn of the Planet of the Apes" I came up with a "Caesar vs. Sassy" incentive. Rather than introduce the incentive the first day of the month along with the other fifty-plus incentives, I found a graphic on Google Images that had huge burgundy curtains around a stage but the curtains were only a third of the way closed. I then borrowed a shot of Caesar, the star ape from the film and reduced it to fit within the drapery opening. Below his picture, I dropped in "vs." and placed a hilarious shot of Sasquatch military pressing two chimps on a long branch below this. In the corner I placed a graphic of a bag of beef jerky. The title of the first teaser was, "Coming Soon: Sassy vs. Caesar – Mini Chimp Incentive." This was then emailed to all of the sales team's iPads, including their division managers all the way up to the president of the company. In the subject box was, "Look what's coming next month…"

I then posted several of these very creative power point pages (they took me about ten to fifteen minutes to create) around the sales office. About a week and a half later I followed up with a second blast to their iPads. This time I grabbed another fierce shot of Caesar on a horse, placing him in the drapery opening above sasquatch who was now (with some creative touch up) holding a bomber bottle of the brewer's IPA in his hand. The sasquatch pic was quite funny. As always there was a bag of beef jerky to the lower right. This time the headline was, "Nearly Here, Are You a Banana or a Jerky Beef?" The reason for the banana mention is not to poke fun at apes, rather it hints at how the team will earn bananas to win an evening with the local brewer rep to go and see the premier of the film – after visiting several supplier-loyal On Premise accounts.

Taking this idea even further I decided to award a higher allocation of "banana points" for distribution on several of the slower moving packages. This way we also made points with our Operations colleagues. Please realize that a night out to the movies does not get street-smart San Francisco sales guys particularly motivated so cash was involved as well as banana point accumulation. That Friday before the incentive began, I must have had ten sales associates including the president of our company inquire about this incentive which I would not mention a word about. I forgot to mention that this incentive was called "mini" because it began on July 1st and ended the following Friday the 11th. This added to the urgency and competitiveness that I wanted to instill around the unique yet supplier-branded incentive.

Just think about how far you could take this nugget of creativity IF your marketing plan and product line were centered around Sasquatch. If so, you would be able to extend the creative strategy down to street level which would allow you to get every cent out of your marketing investment while solidifying a fun position within the marketplace, within the consumer's mind and within the wholesaler's team. This is what few beverage companies realize and miss out on consistently.

As you can see, it is not that hard to come up with something unique and relevant to your brand which should at least be a bit of a creative stretch. This way your audience has fun with your incentive while it boosts much needed awareness ahead of the larger company pack. Remember to make your incentives fun, unique but also relevant to your brand. Make them count or "earn" their contribution to brand equity. Tying these together will reap long term rewards for your marketing efforts.

I recall an incentive I prepared for one of our smallest brewers. They could only afford one per year, so I convinced them to go all in. After determining their goals, we looked at the potential pay out and shared such with the distributor sales manager who appeared as though he was going to be sick. I assured him that we would co-op the incentive which revived him a bit. The incentive, although distribution focused, deserves comment here. I wrote the incentive to play on the dollar values that

95% of all other suppliers levied on new draft handles gained or new package placements achieved in the marketplace. Instead of the standard $100-150 for a new draft handle, we paid out $159.99. For a single SKU placement we paid $6.99, for two SKUs, $14.99 and for three, $22.99. This psychological number-play resonated with the large sales teams so much that whenever they saw a representative from this brewery they called him/her, "$159.99."

The results from this two month incentive were stratospheric. The incentive was supported with a crew drive, six pack post off (discount) and an added incentive that included a VIP dinner for the top salesman and a few of his/her guests at the brew pub...compliments of the brewer. This simple "incentive kicker" was a stroke of brilliance that I remind smaller brewers and vintners of all the time. That is, to exploit your unique strengths. If you have a brewery or vineyard in the distributor's backyard then get their sales teams and management over there! It seems to work best when the sales teams have to **work** for it, but when they win, they love it and the talk value amongst them the following weeks is priceless. This is something that a mega brewer or spirits company cannot match. Rarely does the smaller player have an up on the Fortune 500 corporation. So take advantage of this wisely.

Another example of creative "incentivizing" was taken from bread distributor learnings. When I presented to the route sales teams at 4:30 am while with Earthgrains, I learned that salesmen own their routes and could re-sell them, usually for a tidy profit, after building them up over time. Some routes will stay in a family for generations, used as the family model to ensure a decent living. This got me to thinking about how beverage (beer) guys and gals sell. They too have a route and typically know or have access to the monthly and annual case volume generated from that route. This will be quite a reach from 4:30 am bread sales to beer, but I developed an incentive that I called, "Take Stock in Sam." My goal was to create an enticing incentive that supported the brand's product placement in a feature film while also distinguishing itself from the many five dollar per placement (lackluster) incentives that the sales teams see each and every month.

The incentive was tied to the film, *Wall Street*, starring Michael Douglas. I borrowed several quotes from the film such as "greed is good" and even attempted to impersonate Gordon Gheko in an animated Friday morning sales meeting. This was the first (for me) twelve month incentive that I had ever run in our company. The supplier, Sam Adams, supported it fully.

The logic behind the incentive was this, the route salesman was given the autonomy to earn and sell Sam Adams stock throughout the year. This common stock was fictitious but every sales person received a beginning share quantity and was allowed to trade in their stock at the end of any month of the year. Having taken a forecasting class in my undergraduate studies and learning to enjoy the power behind multiple linear regression, I was able to calculate a mathematical equation that forecasted stock value based on the prior month's volume sales AND distribution placement increases and decreases.

The equation was tested for forecasting accuracy going back twenty four months. With some fine tuning and weighting for distribution I was able to generate a formula that predicted the brand's stock, up or down, on a monthly basis. I then had Sam Adams make us a bunch of formal-looking stock certificates while our graphics team made up a large two by three foot Sam stock ticker. This Sam stock ticker was placed in my office window (across from the men's room which resulted in record "walk by" traffic) where every sales person in the company could see.

With each case placement, draft handle gain and monthly case sales input into the formula, the sales person received shares. That share amount, by route, was made public to them. Once the month's results were in, I paraded through the Friday sales meeting with the massive Sam stock ticker showing the increase in stock value. The rationale behind this grand exercise was the hope that the sales person would take ownership of the brand on their route in an entrepreneurial appeal not attempted by any of the many in-house brands that we sell. Several of the salesmen cashed in their stock within the first four months, however, the majority understood the financial benefit and worked the program through to the end of the year.

I was very pleased at the results (we ended the year up and my forecasts were within 6% accuracy) as most of the sales people either doubled or tripled their Sam brand earnings over prior years which also resulted in record volume and distribution for the brand. I must say that this program did require a lot of work and an extra amount of preselling to one of our senior managers who felt strongly that it was too complicated and that it would fail.

One final consideration on incentives is to try a one week incentive when all other brands are executing monthly, bi-monthly or even quarterly programs. I have seen great success with the infrequently used "mini" incentives which sales teams seem to focus especially hard on. Keep the mini incentive simple, creative and lucrative and you will see results.

The key learning here is to "brand" your incentive in the mind of your sales team audience for ease of recall, execution and differentiation. Develop the incentive around something relevant to your brand, a theme, a special event, a motion picture product placement (like Wall Street II for Sam Adams) a sports sponsorship, an advertising campaign or something. This extra effort will serve to dramatically differentiate your brand's incentive from the many (there can be as many as forty or more supplier incentives each month at the larger wholesalers) others that vie for the sales team's attention.

If done well, you can use this branded incentive over and over so that the sales force will become accustomed to how you incentivize them. I am not advocating simple repetition, I am suggesting that the incentive retain the basic look or feel throughout so that the team quickly embraces the plan and can execute forward based on prior experience with your style. Think about this and your audience. It's similar to hearing BB King play the guitar, you can always tell when he plays his licks. By constantly changing the incentive "look" the result might end up as a diluted attempt that the audience will summarize as just another simple and clone-like incentive to be quickly forgotten.

Remember that street smart sales people will quickly catch on to how little effort you place into a sales incentive. If it is the generic five dollars per placement or a trip to 'Vegas/'Jersey then your "plan" will be dropped to the bottom of the incentive heap. If it truly takes into consideration the audience, is fun, relevant, easy to understand and makes them a lot of money, then it will catapult to the top of the competitive pile and should show better than average sales results for your brand.

XI - DRIVING THE MARKETING PLAN DOWN TO THE WHOLESALER LEVEL

You might be thinking that creative "out of the keg" ideas are a waste of time. If so, you may work for a very large brewer, distillery, and vineyard or water company. In your case, your company may be so big that whatever it needs, it gets, as it wields a mighty financial sword. For the smaller competitor, your creative effort, passion and time are your strategic chinks in the armor of your market share or category leader. In my fifteen plus years working in the distribution and wholesale business, it amazes me how little effort brand teams place into bringing their marketing plan "down" to the distributor level. As a former brand guy, I learned quickly how powerful an army of multiple distributor sales forces can be in disseminating brand communications to BOTH the trade and consumer levels.

Several years ago I met with a large craft brewer's brand manager who was a Harvard graduate. He was supposed to spend the day with me but opted to see San Francisco with his peers then stop by my office for five minutes. We were introduced, and he asked me what his company could do to improve. My single response was to include the distributor sales force in the development and execution of their marketing plan. He was somewhat taken aback by this answer perhaps assuming that I had risen through the ranks as a driver or forklift operator. He thanked me and left my office. I never heard from him again.

Where so many companies miss the boat is when they don't include the distributor in the annual marketing plan. Many large suppliers will fly senior distributor executives to their annual meetings where commercials, new products, new hires and strategies are presented. But does any of this really make it down to the sales man who sees twenty accounts per day? To the merchandiser who places Point-of-Sale in over fifty On and Off Premise accounts per week? To the distributor's graphics department and Brand Manager? Probably not. This is a HUGE fumble which is akin to playing only three quarters of a football game. You've got to finish and finish strong to get the message down to "player" level.

Supplier (i.e., brewer, distiller and vintner) brand managers MUST get out of their offices and hit the road with their sales counterparts and conduct a brand road show complete with Off and On Premise kits that guarantee the execution of the marketing plan. These kits will include the most recent graphics, tag line, product descriptions, wearables, selling examples (including a 30 second elevator pitch on key products), TV ads, radio, Out of Home, web site, Facebook, Twitter, celebrity endorsements, key executive hires (new brew master, for example), demo schedule, IPad downloads, samples, etc. People (your wholesalers) want to be informed and will show their appreciation when they are included. By ignoring this fourth quarter "must do" the marketing team leaves hundreds if not thousands of cases on the table to the competitor that takes this step. A company that does this very well is New Belgium Brewing. They brought their marketing team to a major On Premise account, invited the wholesaler's sales team, gave them lunch and presented the coming year's marketing plan, new packaging, products and social media schedule.

Many companies continue to miss the mark as I have seen many banners, price signs, posters, etc. that did not mention a brand's tag line and often had an old logo. Whose fault is this? The supplier's sales team is not responsible as they are managing the distributor and hopefully making account calls. The dotting of the "Is" and crossing of the "Ts" should be executed by the marketing team. Their job is to ensure that all the marketing creativity and strategy are rolled out to ALL levels, not just wholesaler owners and senior executives. Think about how many pieces of Point of Sale that are hung in accounts every week in this country for your brand. How many banners are made each year for weekend special event placement. Are all these pieces reflecting your current marketing campaign or KDA? Probably not. In fact, probably very few.

Do the sales people know your brand's tag line? Probably not. Is this important? Of course it is! It just might be the only point they remember when they are pitching your new product or brand to their buyer. If the buyer has also been exposed to the campaign then both sides of the equation , Sales and Marketing, are doing their job which will increase the probability of "yes."

As mentioned, supplier brand teams miss a tremendous opportunity by not reflecting their current marketing/advertising campaign down to the distributor sales person level. This critical blunder reveals a lack of strategic foresight by the supplier brand team. Few, if any suppliers take this extra step which is more work to the marketing plan. This opportunity should be addressed as it could leverage important pieces of the brand campaign down to the wholesaler level. By composing a prepared sales incentive that reinforces and syncs with the overall marketing plan, the brand team will get every last drop out of this annual brand investment and have a "keg up" on their competition that simply won't bother. An example of this recommendation might include sports team sponsorships.

If you have negotiated the rights to sponsor a major or minor league team then write an incentive that includes elements for the distributor sales force to rally around such. This might include an evening in a luxury suit, batting practice at the park, a meet and greet with some of the athletes or a sales meeting at the ball park. You can also use this investment to bring out of state distributors via sales incentives designed to achieve volume and/or distribution gains. When reached, the winning team gets to attend an event at this sports venue. This can be a real motivator of wholesalers in "sleepy" geographies that have no major sporting activity. The sponsorship might also include branded glassware that can be sold to On and Off Premise accounts that want to prominently feature this branded point of sale which further reinforces the sponsorship investment.

Product placement is oftentimes a method for subtle brand exposure in TV and cable programming. Think about how huge it would be to write an incentive whereby the top two to four wholesaler salesmen get to appear in that TV commercial. They may just be background "actors" sitting down having one of your beverages but the "talk value" at the distributorship would be phenomenal. This idea could be exploited to pit multiple distributorships against each other. The end product could then be shown to all the teams in their weekly sales meeting to further extend the marketing message to the troops while keeping your brand and campaign miles ahead of any others.

In summary; your distributors and wholesaler teams should be in sync with your marketing plan. Wholesaler sales teams are the troops that can further extend the marketing plan into account nooks and crannies while their graphics and merchandising teams can get those strategic messages into the battlefield (aka appropriate touch points) more adeptly than you might imagine. Use your distributors "synergistically" to rein every dollar invested from your marketing plan.

XII - On vs. Off Premise Distribution

Craft beer and spirits have typically been introduced via the On Premise channel first. This observation is based on consumer trial opportunity as bars are where drinkers can try a new beverage without having to commit to a six pack or full bottle (750 ml) of the beverage. In essence, it is low risk trial with potential positive discovery as the upside. Further, Bart Watson, Brewer's Association economist reported that craft beer accounted for nearly one-third of On Premise dollar sales volume. Regardless of beverage, the On Premise consumer sampling experience will hopefully be remembered when they go into their local grocery store or independent liquor store. Growth for craft beer within the On Premise has been increasing steadily. According to a February 2014 report conducted by Next Level Marketing craft beer bar calls accounted for 12% of beer orders. In 2014 that percentage has grown to 31% while domestic and import beer orders continue their decline[17].

To learn more about the power of the On Premise, a deeper review of this Next Level Marketing article revealed some interesting chain data. This information was compiled from the top twenty five On Premise national chains. These include Buffalo Wild Wings, P.F. Chang's, Red Robin and twenty two others. Here are some key findings[ibid].

> 77% of these chains participate regularly in beverage promotions. The significance here is that your brand should be included in that promotion particularly if it is in the Introduction or Growth Stages of the product life cycle. A discount will be the trial stimulus for the potential new buyer. On this topic, table tents are strongly recommended which should include your brewery or distillery story, several salient copy points about the beers or spirits being offered as well as possible food and desert pairings. Wineries might also consider this option.

> 82% of these chains conduct regular happy hours. As mentioned, reducing the price during higher traffic hours represents a tremendous trial opportunity to get your brands into the mouths of potential new customers.

> On Premise chain buyers are interested in unique drinks that consumers can't get anywhere else. If you are a specialty brand, then carefully pick your On Premise accounts and try to help them with their differentiating

strategy. This partnership will empower your relationship with the account. Train these accounts to understand that your brands help to support/complement their bars' brand positioning and overall product portfolio.

The typical draft beer menu includes 19% domestic beer (down from 38% in 2009), 22% Imports (down from 29%) while craft beer jumped from 33% to 59% in the same time span. This means that these top twenty five chains devote roughly six out of every ten draft lines to craft! This increase is quite promising for the craft brewer and should be viewed as consumer "voting" (aka demand) for more craft beer in the On Premise channel. With the upswing in crafts and interest in select imports, such as Modelo and Heineken, these "power chains" which include; Chili's and Ruby Tuesday's, are focusing more on craft beer styles.

Based on Guest Metrics data, a market research firm that specializes in capturing trends in the On Premise, when a patron orders a craft beer in a restaurant, the average check is $80 vs. an average check associated with Budweiser of $63[18]. That means that by serving craft brands, restaurants can expect check averages to increase by as much as 27%. Further, Guest Metrics found that the highest check average came when Heineken (Dutch import) was purchased resulting in an impressive $89 check average. These are compelling findings and should certainly be used as "selling ammunition" by craft and import sales representatives when calling on local and national restaurants and chains.

According to Guest Metrics LLC, when comparing the first three quarters of 2012 against the same period in 2011, craft beers experienced rapid growth in the on-premise channel. According to Guest Metrics CEO, Bill Pecoriello, during that time period, craft beer sales grew 10.7% from the prior year, while imports contracted by -1.3%, premium light beers by -1.6%, and premium regular beers by -2.9%. This double digit gain for crafts reflects impressive On Premise consumer demand that can be exploited by supplier and wholesaler sales reps. This is significant growth considering the fourth quarter is craft's best-selling in the entire year.

On the subject of craft beer, Guest Metrics LLC, found that India Pale Ale was the prominent call of craft beer choice in

2012 displaying the strongest unit growth which was up 39% for the year (!). Largest IPA brand share increases came from brands Widmer, Ballast Point, Sierra Nevada and Lagunitas. Conversely, Pale Ale and Lagers shrank 5% in 2012 despite being the largest beer type with a 33% share of all beer sold. Two of the largest share losers included Bud Light and Budweiser[19].

To put this into perspective, there are nearly 20,000 brands of beer (3,000 are craft, 1,000 of which are defined as "new"), wine and spirits all competing for share of stomach in the On Premise channel[20]. This competition underscores the importance of heeding the recommendations made in this book for the small to medium brewer, distiller or vintner. The blog also shared that craft beers experienced strong growth in 2012 capturing 1.3% unit share at the expense of premium light, import and premium regular beers. Further, 25% of all craft beer is consumed On Premise.

When studying On Premise pricing, Guest Metrics LLC, divided craft draught beers into four tiers[21]. Tier 1, the most expensive craft beer accounting for 19% of craft beer unit sales grew 27% vs. just 3% for the other three tiers which accounted for 81% of all craft beer sold On Premise. Tier II represented 36%, Tier III 26% and Tier IV 20% of unit sales[22]. Tier 1 beers had an average price of $6.65; 20 to 50% higher than the other three tiers. This may provide some insight into On Premise pricing strategy which should appease your On Premise buyer from a margin perspective. It also hints at a long held consumer corollary that higher quality products justify a higher price and are therefore worth buying because the need satisfaction return will be higher. This premiumization fact, according to Guest Metrics[ibid], is similar to that found in the wine and spirits categories.

Lastly, a Nielsen report, stated that crafts skew heavily On Premise with greater than half of dollars spent there on craft. Nielsen also found that 27% of beer drinkers like to try beer at bars and 60% of that group will then buy in-store (Off Premise) if they like the product[23].

Over the past twenty to thirty years, the wine industry has not done a particularly good job of educating consumers on the great variety of wines that come from all over the world. Perhaps therein lies the problem: there are just too many wine styles, brands, price points, sizes, etc. Who would not be intimidated by this vast array of options? The industry is doing a better job at educating consumers but this might be the chink in the armor that craft beer needs to attack. Craft beer's image is that of fun, trust, discovery, quality, refreshment, socializing and friendship. This observation is supported by Charles Gill, CEO of Wine Metrics, who agrees that craft beer is taking share from wine. How are they doing it? Via innovation, promotion, new traditions, customer loyalty, food compatibility and other methods[24].

Wisely, retailers are now reducing wine real estate in favor of craft and high end import beers with good reason. Beer marketers continue to see opportunity to beat wine at retail via food pairings in the On Premise portion of the business. Brewer dinners are now common and strongly suggested as a method to engage potential buyers in an intimate (soft sell) setting. Another popular and successful tactic is the tap takeover which allows consumers to sample a wide variety of beers supplied by one brewery. A word of caution is that a brewery representative MUST always attend these tap takeovers to ensure that consumer questions about the brand are answered accurately. Try your best to avoid a wholesaler stand in who may not share the passion or knowledge level needed to best present your brands.

Another method to win potential On Premise real estate is via private label production. Many retailers are looking for craft beers and wines to place in their restaurants, hotels and bars as their own. This relationship can help cover manufacturing costs or it might even be a solid path to take to satisfy primary craft demand. Once in the account with private label draft, a relationship can flourish resulting in branded draft opportunity down the road. Private label Off Premise packages are also in demand at the retail level. Most retailers don't mind if the producer comes in with a branded product on top of the private label that might already be selling well.

Hotels and the On Premise – Forgotten Opportunity?

Beer Business Daily published a special report titled, "Beer in Hotels[25]." This insightful piece merits consideration. The editors of BBD are "very bullish on hotels," and with good reason. Their analysis revealed that both food and beverage hotel channel sales have been on an upward swing through and are forecasted to rise through the next few years. Further, according to Technomic, a consumer On Premise research firm, consumer revenue spent on alcoholic beverages within the hotel segment rose 6% while case volume increased 3%. Technomic predicts revenue to climb by 5.6% and case volume to continue to rise by 2.5% per year[ibid]. This often misunderstood segment holds great potential for your beverage brands.

So how big is the alcoholic beverage hotel pie? The special report stated that Hotels represented 8% or **$7.4 billion** of the overall $86.3 billion market (yes that is B for billion)[ibid]. Interestingly, the report stated that Hotels under index in alcoholic product consumption when compared to casual dining, bars and nightclubs. A Beer Marketer's Insight newsletter reported from On Premise research firm, Technomic, that the hotel/lodging industry accounts for 7.2% of all On Premise beer sales[26]. Moreover, half of hotel operators reported their alcohol sales are growing and to support such that they will be placing more focus on their bar business. The report went on to state that 33% of 21 to 34-year olds visit a hotel at least once per month vs. just 14% of those 35 or older. As a result, "hotel operators are realizing a creative and operationally-sound drink program executed across the various outlets of a hotel property can add value and enhanced experience elements for guests, as well as high-profit sales[ibid]."

The Technomic's Bar TAB report optimistically projected a 4% increase in food and beverage sales through 2014. What does that mean for your brand(s)? Opportunity as consumers staying at hotels have increased their beverage consumption by 35% for craft and import beers.

How do you take advantage of this channel growth? By targeting hotels within your distribution network that further support your brand positioning and sales objectives. It is important to understand this statement as a Belgian-style brewer of 750 ml double abbey would not want their brand available in a discount motel. Once these "brand appropriate" hotels are identified, the next step is to send in one of your reps along with your distributor sales person to present the above findings. Once you have the buyer interested; then present your brands, concepts, such as tap takeovers, bucket deals, draft programs like, "Taste the Locale," and food pairings/beer dinners, etc. This is an excellent channel for 21 to 34-year olds to discover your brand! Don't forget to ask for a piece of the "mini fridge" business as well. You may also consider a private label draft program which could lead to bigger and better opportunities with the account in the future. Volume success via this private label concept might be used to pitch other accounts to further expand your business.

Many beverage suppliers ignore the hotel/motel segment perhaps assuming that it is left to multi-thousand SKU foodservice specialty distributors. Or perhaps there is a lack of understanding or appreciation for this relatively unknown foodservice channel. Some reps prefer to leave the hotels to national managers who call on the chains at their headquarters. This is fine as long as the brands are poured and available, however, there are thousands of hotels who could use your products to increase their total revenue and will show their appreciation for your consulting partnership. The compounded annual growth rate for the segment through 2017 is forecasted to be 3.1% which represents an exceptional growth area for refined account-by-account targeting. For small to medium sized brands who may be getting shut down by bigger brands in mainstream retail, high profile channels such as sports bars, nightclubs, arenas, pubs/taverns, casinos and gentleman's clubs; the hotel segment represents an excellent channel to pursue with great vigor.

XIII- BRAND PROLIFERATION and the CONSEQUENCES of UNBRIDLED PRODUCT SEGMENTATION

"...*there continues to be a rapid brand proliferation in the number of beers sold, which is up 21% thus far*" said Bill Pecoriello, CEO of Guest Metrics commenting on core brand performance vs. innovation in the industry[27]. To get an idea of what is to come, I think it relevant to review the past and how marketing has helped influence the retail and product introduction landscape.

The Industrial Revolution - the Early 1900's

With the advent of the iron horse, locomotives traversed across this great nation carrying with them large volumes of goods that helped fuel the Industrial Revolution. Unfortunately, the prosperity was short-lived with the onslaught of the Great Depression of the 1930's. After the country pulled out of its doldrums, a "Production Orientation" took hold of the United States in the 1940's and beyond. Here is an excellent definition of the concept:

> "The production orientation assumes that consumers will prefer product based on its quality, performance and innovative features. This means that the company knows its product better than anyone or any organization. Thus, the company knows what will work in designing and producing the product and what will not work. Since the company has the great knowledge and skill in making the product, it also assumes it knows what is best for the consumer. The product concept compelled companies to ensure improving product quality and introduce new features to enhance product performance. This was done without consulting the customer to find his or her view on these product features. Yet, products were produced with the customer in mind. Since the era culminated development of innovative products which did not have substitutes, customer needs might not be too much a demand since customers may not know their needs in such an innovative market situation. In much of the production era, organizations were able to sell all of the products that they made. The success of this philosophy was due mostly to the time and level of technology in which it was dominant. The product concept survived well after the Industrial Revolution. Since demand exceeded supply, the emphasis on production rather than the customer was quite an appropriate business thought at the time.

Most goods were in such short supply that companies could sell all that they made. Consequently, <u>organizations did not need to consult with consumers about designing and producing their products</u>. Much as some companies may still have a product oriented business thinking that directs their operations, the concept is not popular in today's business environment. A product philosophy often leads to the company focusing on the product rather than on the consumer needs that must be satisfied. With the nature of customers and business environment the product philosophy might be a failure today, except for the introduction of new products where there may be insufficient customer knowledge and competition[28]."

As the United States prospered through the late 1940's, particularly after the end of World War II, the Detroit auto industry rode the "production orientation highway" for some thirty or more years. Back then, Detroit, known as the "Big Three" (FORD, General Motors and Chrysler) had a stranglehold on the US automotive industry. These auto manufacturers dictated to US consumers what cars should be; big, heavy, unreliable, gas guzzlers with V-8 engines. Economists and marketers recognized and accepted this production orientation model, which was the norm for this period. Demand for goods was so strong after the war that manufacturers sold everything they could make. Across the board, inventories were constantly sold out. But a marketing orientation was not far off.

For over three decades, Detroit enjoyed telling US consumers what they wanted, when they wanted it and how much they would pay for it. Not until the seventies, when the US experienced a devastating fuel crisis, did the US automotive *oligopoly* get a scare from Japan that would change the course of this goliath industry, then the world's largest - forever. Monitoring Detroit ever so closely, DAT Motorcar Company, a Japanese automotive manufacturer of the Datsun, now called Nissan, began exporting B-210s, Bumble Bees and 240Z cars from 1965-1975 that achieved incredible gas mileage (for the time); a consumer benefit shunned by the Big Three. DAT's strategy, according to former President of North American Nissan operations, Yutaka Katayama, was to, "improve their car's efficiency; gradually, and creep up slowly before others noticed. Then, before Detroit realizes it, we (DAT) will have become an excellent car maker, and the customers will think so too[29]." Detroit, however, ignored Japan's inroads with resultant devastating market share effect. As a result, today's automotive landscape is far changed from decades ago as Asian and European automakers dominate many aspects of the US market. So what does this have to do with beer? A lot.

As the nation's appetite for goods and services began to level out, some manufacturers recognized the need to shift away from the production orientation into a marketing orientation. Champions of the marketing concept realized that they had to change – because of competition (like Japan forced upon Detroit in the automotive example) AND because they learned that it was better for their business models to satisfy consumer wants and needs, rather than dictate to them. So does your company practice a production or a marketing orientation? The answer to this question should be outlined in the corporate marketing plan. Once you have decided which orientation your company will support (I suggest marketing), then you will be able to better understand your competition by identifying and exploiting their weaknesses.

"Retail Evolution"

As Detroit's business model was threatened by the Japanese, so too did the US food and drink environment begin to change. This change was not due to foreign competition but to technological improvements, which would be later exploited by the goliath consumer packaged goods companies. The industry really took off "intellectually" with the advent of the Universal Product Code or UPC. The UPC, designed by IBM, and first used in a Marsh Supermarket in Troy, Ohio on June 26, 1974 (the first scanned item was a pack of Wrigley's Juicy Fruit gum)[30] was designed to reduce human cashier input error and lower price tagging labor hours by supermarket personnel.

Other benefits included making the product buyer and inventory managers' lives much easier while it provided rapid feedback on sales per product slot performance. In the late seventies, large research companies such as AC Nielsen and International Research Institute (IRI) recognized the selling revenue and the supplier and retailer benefits of capturing, dissecting and analyzing this information. Retailers agreed to sell this raw purchase data to Nielsen and IRI who in turn resold it, after some massaging, to manufacturers, distributors, importers, brokers, publishers and suppliers. The manufacturers then shared the results with their marketing, R & D and sales teams. The sales teams then cherry-picked this data as their bible to be used in countless power point presentations, all pointing a finger at slow moving competitive products while highlighting their growing stars.

The data has been used in countless ways to influence retailers and others within the industry. New terms were introduced including All Commodity Volume (ACV) which is a measure of distribution within supermarket stores selling over a required dollar threshold per week. In my opinion, the use of this data is excellent when making category management decisions, which in effect should guard against product cannibalism. ACV also helps to identify distribution voids when introducing a new item or brand. These voids can be quickly plugged by the local distributors who can't hide from these glaring out of stocks. I, however, feel that many large food and beverage companies often use these numbers to frame a biased landscape with which to sell from and to persuade retail buyers. The reliance on these monthly, quarterly and annual numbers, and on their selective presentation formatting, may have brain-washed many in our respective industries. You may think that I have overindulged in a few too many IPAs, but let me explain.

The UPC and its associated data mining have been with us for over forty years. When we accept this powerful data as the industry standard we put ourselves into a position of naiveté. As a former marketing research analyst, I caution against fully accepting UPC data as the absolute standard from which many critical decisions are made. Here's why. UPC data can be manipulated by a savvy consumer packaged goods company to create consumption indexes. Products are then produced according to perceived "gaps" in those indexes.

For example, let's assume an index of average beer consumption is 100. We will operationalize this as the "domestic" or average beer drinker. An index of 130 could be deemed appropriate for a consumer group that might have a higher propensity to buy a craft IPA instead of a domestic beer. Conversely, an index of less than 100, might indicate a consumer segment's strong preference for a malt based, lemonade product. What I am alluding to is how an over-zealous brewer might use, or bias, data to support their constant flow of product line extensions. In my opinion, the goliath brewer's model harkens back to a production orientation (Detroit) using data to justify brewer-contrived product gaps in the retailer's shelf or cooler offering. Producing products to fill these gaps, called needs/wants by their sophisticated sales and category management teams, ensures shelf space dominance and retailer support.

Is manipulating UPC data, therefore, the optimum methodology to produce then introduce new items to the market? Once the over-zealous brewer has convinced the retailer that this fabricated landscape of unserved product opportunity exists, based on the UPC-derived numbers, then they will continue to win the shelf space battle while appeasing their many stockholders. And for marginal selling products that slump on the shelves, they have dozens in line waiting (picture in your mind the mother Alien from the science fiction film, spewing out thousands of "six pack" eggs) for this space, supported with "industry standard" numerical rationale, category captainship and extravagant marketing budgets. Some of the consumer packaged goods goliaths have built the pool to play in but are not inviting anyone to swim. Have they been successful in convincing the retailers? Not totally, but as a classically trained marketing research analyst, I question the use of quantitative historical data instead of qualitative methods for the introduction of new products which I feel contributes to fabricated or contrived demand.

It is clear to me, therefore, that many of the large consumer packaged goods companies use UPC data to support an outdated Product Orientation model rather than a pro-consumer, Marketing Orientation, practiced by today's craft brewers. Despite this allegiance to a marketing orientation, are things going to get better for the small to medium sized brewers, vintners and distillers? Far from it as the stakes are sky-high.

Product Segmentation – More to Choose From

The beer industry, in my opinion, is not mimicking the wine segment, as some point out today, rather I see it evolving more similarly to the soft drink industry of the '80's. In the late '70's, the soft drink industry was, and still is, dominated by Coke and Pepsi with a sprinkling of regional and local brands that vied for the "left overs" that Coke and Pepsi let them have, what I refer to as the "shelf scraps." During that time period, the food and beverage category undertook a remarkable change as entrepreneurs recognized opportunity through market segmentation. Although not in the beverage business and I doubt that he was the first, Orville Redenbacher really got the American consumer interested in what was always perceived as a commodity – that being popcorn! He actually got Americans to pony up nearly double the price for his company's, "premium, gourmet popcorn," and it was worth it.

The soft drink industry took notice, expanding or segmenting with the likes of diet sodas, double caffeinated colas such as Jolt and healthier (and higher priced) soft drinks from brands like Hansen's Beverage targeting a more affluent demographic while expanding or segmenting the category. Private label brands, meanwhile appealed to the economy-conscious.

Segmentation, a marketing term that refers to refined market slicing into smaller and smaller homogeneous sub-markets,[31] could be seen across many product categories in the eighties. Segmentation was particularly evident in the ice cream business, even more so with the advent of the pint category. Who would have thought that American would ever consider deviating from their gallon container of vanilla ice cream that deemed to have a lock in America's freezers.

Not until marketers dreamed up faux import brands like Frusen Gladje and Haagen Dazs, and "local" brands like Ben and Jerry's, Steve's and Honey Hill Farms Premium Frozen Yogurt, did Americans come to embrace the newly created super premium pint category. Was this category based on UPC data gaps? No, it was based on demand for better quality ice cream and the notion that it is better to eat a little of something really good than to eat a lot of something marginal. But would consumers pay as much as five dollars for a pint of ice cream? Indeed yes! Move over ice cubes, your vanilla now has a neighbor or two. Brilliant marketers behind brands like Ben and Jerry's, helped pave the way to impressive margins, product assortment and better quality consumables for all of us. But what happens when you go too far?

Consequences – Segmentation on Hyper Drive

Today's beer business is sharply over segmented. Many warn against this "SKU-centric" proliferation/phenomenon which some of us refer to as, "SKUmegedon." Some trade groups are reporting that there may be as many as five thousand breweries in the US by the end of 2016. The consequences? Shelf and draft handle saturation. Meanwhile, some of the world's largest brewers are the biggest perpetuators of this trend, repeating the practice that Coke and Pepsi did back in the eighties. When the upstart soft drink brands began appearing on small to medium-sized supermarket chain shelves, Coke and Pepsi introduced dozens of product line extensions which served to flex or block all potential competition, regardless of the cannibalism rate.

This bloated extension of product line introductions was the precursor to the science of category management. Back then and today, the goliaths of the industry, incur this planned and budgeted for (a cost of doing business and on balance sheets) cannibalism profit hit as giant conglomerates simply wait out their smaller competitors. A Pepsico regional manager admitted to me in an interview that Pepsi will incur cannibalism in favor of maintaining a competitive image including setting trends with new products or paralleling competitive entries from the likes of Coca Cola, Dr. Pepper or 7-Up. At this big league level, the pressure for large beverage companies to maintain innovation and match competitive offerings, forces them to introduce new products in order to guarantee market position[32].

On the subject of product cannibalism, Kerrin, Harvey and Rothe were credited with identifying three distinctive definitions[33], however, I see a fourth, what I call, "exploitive cannibalism." This pre planned strategy of, "SKU clogging" is here to stay as brewing goliaths are poised to over segment nearly every conceivable beverage niche from light beer and malt liquor to cider and mead. This threatening trend won't change soon as giant brewers exert shelf category dominance while oftentimes under cutting their competition from a pricing advantage via scanning or other method.

Understand that two brewers control 75% of the beer volume in the United States and have fought long and hard to achieve this market share. Moreover, they now view the craft segment as theirs to take. Their immensity and relationships at the major supermarket, drug and On Premise chain levels will make entry into these channels particularly frustrating for the small to medium brands all vying for the same shelf space or draft handles. So for many of these 5,000 new brands, they will have to find alternative locations to sell their beers.

The mega brewer's model fosters and promotes the introduction of new items at an alarming pace. The new product onslaught will bring "temporary SKUs" to the shelves, born with fractional product life cycles. Supporting this model, the giant brewers have an infinite line of extensions and new products strategically designed to preserve shelf space into infinium.

The shelf dominance strategy was corroborated in a national wholesaler meeting whereby one of the mega brewer's management laid out their future brand plans. These plans, for example, included the announcement of a new found category, dubbed, "alcofusion." The category was described in a Beer Business Daily newsletter[34] as neither liquor nor beer, but born of "sociability." This is a prime example of fabricating a demand gap in UPC category data while blocking space from beverage competitors.

In the "category" exists the Limearita. This brand includes peach, cranberry, raspberry and mango all lined up, just waiting for the green light in eight, sixteen and twenty five ounce package sizes. Competitors are exasperated with this product introduction strategy with SKUs that succumb to a, "Mayfly-like" product life cycle. These products seem to hit their decline stage with the finesse of a cheap bottle rocket but the pipeline fill is so addicting to the big retailers that they continue to authorize this "Gatling Gun" new product approach. Yet there is more on the way as domestic beer consumption continues to falter. As a result, large brewers are laying off hundreds of employees. Could this plethora of new products be a result of desperation? Not hardly. This is how some brewers operate, this is the Big Leagues. Where will the space come from for this plethora of new products? This real estate will have to come from somewhere...

"Bully Beer" - What does this SKU clogging trend mean for the small to medium brewer?

Another significant issue is the mega brewer's insistence on keeping products firmly on the downside of the Maturity phase of their product life cycle, that is, sleeping on store shelves. Because of their distribution mass, these "senior citizen, homeless on the park shelf" products will continue to generate some level of volume. Rather than discontinue (disco or D-code) these lifeless and declining brands, millions of dollars will be thrown at them attempting to "re curve" the product's life cycle or "restoring the core" by changing the product's bottle color, size, label, dispensing diameter or some other gimmick that appeases the retailer and further blocks a product or brand, such as a craft or import, from gaining needed retailer space.

On the plus side, for the small guys, re curve marketing strategies will gradually backfire further leaching whatever brand equity may be left. This will not happen overnight but I suggest studying what has become of the Michelob brand over the years and how it now languishes in the decline stage of its product life cycle, belching off marginal quality product line extensions, many at $3.99 per six pack price points. Recall that this was THE super-premium US beer brand many years ago. Now with the success of Michelob Ultra, the brand name basically means "diet beverage" as they affix the sleepy marque to an Ultra cider, that takes up more space on the shelf.

What can the small guy do? The savvy craft brewer must battle for this chain space with a well-trained, educated and prepared top notch presenter to call on these chain buyers and convince them of the merits of their brands and why they deserve some of the space dominated by the multi-national with their low margin brands and clone-like extensions. Supporting your line with the many recommendations made within this book such as local community special event participation/sponsorship and picking seasoned distributors that know these chain buyers (and the liquor-floor, individual store clerks) will increase your probability of success as competition for this precious real estate escalates to fever pitch level. The retailers have the acreage. The question is: Do they want to grow weeds or roses?

A final point for the upstart brand is to maintain price. To entice their price sensitive target market, the giant brewers habitually offer price discounts and/or brand support via "bar bucks" which further discounts their brands. The craft brewer must resist the temptation to reduce price which will stick in the minds of retail buyers (Off and On Premise) who realize and know that higher quality beverages cost more because they have higher quality ingredients in them. This low price introduction tactic unfortunately, often helps the mega brewer by further locking in precious shelf space.

As a result, the multi-national factory brewers, therefore, act as shelf bullies lining up an endless array of product extensions affording the cannibalism hit in favor of shelf space and draft handle real estate preservation. In essence, these brands act as interior linemen blocking the shelf from smaller craft brands. The strategy is akin to killing off the brand as it begins to peak through its growth stage of the product life cycle in favor of another "new and improved" brew. This perpetual plant, harvest and re-plant farming cycle preserves finite shelf space for the parent company while denying access to higher margin and higher quality beers such as crafts. This "grand fathered in" dominance can also be seen at major sporting event coliseums and concert venues where the mega brewers clearly have the majority of selling opportunity.

Fighting Back

The craft brewer can't sit and take it but must passionately <u>challenge the Detroit model</u> built by the behemoth brewers which is constantly driven home by their sales team armies who take up full time residence under the retailer's roofs. I am referring to the Category Management squads that work full time at retailer headquarters "helping" their analysts to interpret IRI and Nielsen data for the benefit of both teams. This relationship includes account "captaincy" which gives the giant brewers shelf assignment and dictating rights during crucial trimester shelf and cooler resets. This power is ominous and final.

Having been a consumer packaged goods category manager, I know firsthand how numbers are used to a brand's benefit. I also learned the power of winning over a major retailer's category team to the benefit of my employer. Once a schematic is agreed to, then drawn up, that document represents the "shelf real estate bible." If deviated from at store level, the one responsible for the change will incur the wrath of the retailer for some time (referred to as being in the penalty box). This wrath can result in millions of dollars in lost revenue or worse...

I see the goliath brewers as companies that steadfastly subscribe to the aged product orientation concept. Conversely, I see the small to medium-sized craft brewer as the champion of the marketing concept which evolved after companies graduated from a production orientation to that of a marketing orientation. This was due in part to competition but more so because it was better to satisfy consumer needs and wants, rather than dictate them. Do the mega brewers introduce products based on legitimate needs or wants? Not so much. They take a GLOBAL "liquids" model perspective on behalf of their stockholders who are their priority, not consumers. <u>Consumers, therefore, are a by-product of successful production orientation execution.</u> Stock growth is job one with today's huge consumer packaged goods companies. They all have many stockholders to appease.

Conversely, product quality and a satisfied consumer are job one for the craft brewer, vintner and distiller. As you can see, this is where you can fight back, the groups have two very different "bosses" to report to. What currently exists therefore, is a significant philosophical difference between supporting a production vs. a marketing orientation. Herein lies the true chink in the giant's armor. If you want to beat these formidable competitors, study how they go to market via their adherence to their model and how they "use" UPC data to their advantage. For the sake of example, consider them as Detroit and the craft brewers as Japan. Dick Yuengling, fifth generation brewer at Yuengling and Sons summed it up nicely in the 2009 film, "Beer Wars, Brewed in America" by Anat Baron when he said that, "people are fed up with corporate America jamming down the consumer's throat what they want to." The Craft Brewer must never give up the fight.

We have spent a great deal of ink on how the world's largest develop, launch and manage new products. They have done so for decades with phenomenal success. But what is the craft brewer's methodology for bringing a new product to market? Are these decisions based on numerical data gaps? Do the small brewers pay for the IRI or Nielsen scan data, study it and determine that there is an opening, or "unmet need" for a dry-hopped, Imperial India Pale Ale? No, they brew products based on passion, brew pub consumer reaction, bartender input, <u>customer wants</u>, tasting panel feedback, and the love for what they do and their craft. This is the significant difference between the long-established mega brewer and the craft brewer who does not have thousands of stockholders to answer to and impress.

Practicing a production orientation, the mega brewer must focus on maximizing profitability to their shareholders by generating sales, even if it means inventing products for which no consumer demand will ever exist. Read the words of one of the mega brewer's top marketing executives on new brand philosophy which supports my advice, "We're planning to invest for success. What that means is that we have done substantial analysis to understand what marketing investment is required to be successful based on a number of different metrics. We have looked at our previous launches, at our competitor's launches and determined what the right spend is, and that is what we are going to spend off these two platforms[35]."

This is certainly not "craft speak." Notice not one mention of "customer" or "wants/needs" but four mentions of "we." Much can be learned from this quote (which sounds more like stockholder appeasement) by the upstart craft brewer. These sentences reveal a sophisticated model that the giant brewers use to force feed the marketplace with mash tun loads of undifferentiated items. Does increasing the can diameter by 1/32 of an inch or adding one more ounce to a 24 ounce can constitute a new SKU therefore requiring more space allocated for such? Does it deserve to be on the shelf despite a $100 million investment? Is there relevant and valid demand for this merry-go-round of fractionally modified commodity liquid? I don't think so and it is the craft brewer's job to convince the retailer or bar owner otherwise, or they will lose this battle.

How to Win – Chippin' Away

Despite the hundreds of clone products hitting today's shelves, there is an avenue for the craft brewer to consider. That is with a strategy of targeted account distribution. By generating a list of accounts relevant to your brand, then tenaciously going to every one of those accounts, determined to gain placement. The craft brewer will need to keep this geography very tight and manageable. The temptation to cover a large area will be defeatist. This focused strategy will bypass the large supermarket chains, for now.

The best strategy I have seen is when a major city or metropolitan area is divided up amongst its relevant neighborhoods. Reps then descend upon each selected neighborhood striking off each account that they win over. Once the authorization goal is achieved, they progress to the next neighborhood. By the end of the month they can end up with over one hundred solid and relevant "up and down the street" account placements. The sales results, or "pull," from these stores should then be documented for future supermarket buyer presentations.

Savvy small company brewers and distillers will need to decide whether or not the big supermarket battle is one that they want to participate/compete in. It may become too expensive to compete for this channel as the giant brewers continue their blocking strategy against the medium and smaller craft upstarts. That is not to say that good business can't be had in the On Premise and up and down the street classes of trade, quite the contrary! A major metropolitan city can easily derive a majority of its volume from the General Market (sometimes referred to as "Indies" for independents) and the On Premise due to a lack of real estate in crowded urban areas. These tightly built cities do not have the space for large supermarkets, which can be advantageous for the craft brewer.

Another way to battle the impending beer and package monsoon will be to brew high quality seasonal or thematic beers that will catch the attention of the supermarket buyer. These custom seasonals will serve to further differentiate your brand from huge brewer clone extensions. A fine example of this tactic is Anchor Steam's Christmas Ale which has reached cult status in many markets and is now a holiday tradition at many US dining tables throughout the fourth quarter holiday season. Smaller brands searching for a chink in the goliath brewer armor might consider something like a, "Santa's Chimney Slide Ale" in a single serve bomber (22 ounce) or corked 750 ml bottle to gain "authorization rapport" with the retail buyer. If the Christmas product sells successfully then the brewer might get more face time with that supermarket buyer in the coming year. THIS is how you begin to win, slowly and methodically. That brewer might then specialize in tight window seasonals or "brewed and named around thematic periods or holidays."

Recall years ago when Jones Soda introduced their limited production, "Turkey and Gravy" soda for Thanksgiving. The cases were so popular that they sold on E Bay for hundreds of dollars each. Creative, tenacious smaller brewers can learn from this case history and from Anchor Brewing. Just think of the creative options – "Turkey Gobbler Stout, Dracula's Red Lambic, Honey Bunny Easter Egg Hefe, President's Day Porter, Fourth of July American Pale Ale, etc." These unique beers would all be brewed in limited quantity around a brief selling window imparting a sense of urgency upon the targeted consumer. Monitor this suggestion for reality in your markets. Keep in mind that craft seasonal dollar shares were up 12.6% representing nearly a fifth (19.7%) of the entire craft beer business[36]. This "one and done" tactic may not seem like the best way to grow your business but it represents a significant in-road to this most challenging and rewarding channel of the beverage industry.

As mentioned, it might also get your brewery on the buyer's radar. Be sure to support the new brew with qualitative research results such as tasting panel input or brew pub focus group-like requests for the beer. You could include Go Pro video comments from live consumers as they taste the beer at your brewery/tasting room or at a business networking function or beer festival. Now this is creative (and inexpensive) marketing that syncs with sales! This creative content would also help differentiate your brand personality from other beers or beverages all chasing after the same customer. Don't cower but actively challenge IRI and Nielsen numbers then show the buyers your videos of actual consumers, not numbers or indexes, but real, live humans discovering, loving, consuming, interacting and BUYING YOUR beverage. Exploit your brand personality to your authorization advantage and use the UPC argument as an intellectual base to sell against. Can the Crafts "de-brain wash" the retailers?

Rather than analyzing the market from a pricing standpoint, accretive product lineup or index gap perspective, craft brewers should brew products based on want and need consumer satisfaction. Craft brewers must brew based on market reaction as opposed to market dictation. The "Crafts" therefore, need to challenge the mega brewer model at Chain level and convince the chain buyers and category managers to authorize valid products based on wants and needs rather than pseudo-liquids, marketed to fill fabricated index gaps. This battle will not be an easy one and needs to be fought at a higher organized level than just by the individual craft brewer.

On this topic, the upstart brewer should also remind the chain retailer about freshness and how many of the huge brewer product line extensions sit on the shelves barely pulling a case per month (please refer to Amy Gutierrez, Beverages and More buyer interview in the appendix on this topic). This can, and oftentimes leads to old beer which will translate to diminishing retailer revenue and retail shelf slot inefficiency. It will also leave a bad taste in the consumer's mouth as they realize that the retailer that they frequent sells old beer. This in turn may lead them away to a retail competitor. Try to get this (competitive old beer) information to the supermarket chain category manager. Your distributor can be an ally here as they are in the stores almost daily. You might task some of your street reps to monitor a specific competitive package watching for shelf movement or a lack there of (go ahead and stake out that real estate). These facts can then be included in your supermarket buyer presentation, oftentimes, with great effectiveness.

Having taught undergraduate and graduate level marketing management and strategy for twelve years, I scoured many a textbook for just the right case study to make key points to my students. One of those cases I used often is relevant to you. That case is Lestoil.

Jacob Barowsky was a Harvard-educated Russian immigrant who settled on the East Coast. He worked in the dry cleaning industry where he noticed significant cleaning agent deficiencies. In a baby's bathtub, he and chemist John Tulenko came up with their first batch of liquid synthetic detergent called Lestoil. Sounds a bit like a craft brewer story doesn't it? The name Lestoil was derived from the names of his three children. The product initially was sold to commercial laundries and dry cleaners, to paper mills and to factories that required industrial-level cleaning.

During World War II, there were significant shortages of soap materials which provided Barowsky with an entrée into the consumer goods market. At first he was reluctant to take on goliath competitors like Procter and Gamble and Lever Bros, the "goliath brewers" of the soap business. These two corporate giants controlled grocery shelf space (sound somewhat familiar?), however, Barowsky was a fighter and developed a strategy that would change the course of consumer goods marketing for years to come.

Mr. Barowsky's success strategy was simple yet brilliant. What he did was pre-seed individual major metro marke.st with advertising then have sales people visit retailers making presentations and leaving Lestoil samples. He also insisted on fair trade pricing refusing to discount the brand. Instead of subscribing to the typically aggressive expansion model into as many new markets as possible, he opted for a slow motion saturation strategy that generated market share by the case load, one market at a time. Although not recommended for the craft brewer, his use of television advertising to pre seed the distribution territory covered was ingenious. This strong form of "pull promotion" worked to gain retailer attention at the expense of the goliath competitors. In today's marketing mix option bucket, craft brewers could use social media and beer festival samplings to garner excitement around their brands poised to enter a market, or to expand into another.

After the market had been exposed to Lestoil via media, Mr. Barowsky then ensured that his sales team, including himself, would personally visit the retailers for the buy in. This market-by-market additive approach represents a potent strategy for the small to medium-sized craft brewer, distiller or vintner to gain market entry into a major metro. Under Mr. Barowsky's model, resources were concentrated and directed at larger competitors to outmaneuver or neutralize them, provided they were directed at one market only. Although this market by market strategy is much slower than with an immediate commitment to national or regional distribution, the risks are reduced while the tactic more practical for smaller firms.

The lesson is to maximize your brand presence one market at a time bringing all resources to bear on that market while gaining substantial and attainable levels of distribution before even considering another. This case history also shows the benefit of a deep relationship with the local wholesaler getting the brand to a solid, initial footing rather than spraying it across multiple geographies. It is equally important to study how Mr. Barowsky oversaw the retail relationships made at each and every level of his business. By forming strong alliances within a tight geography, he assured himself of brand growth and success[37].

The Lestoil example is somewhat similar to how Jim Koch started his firm; Boston Beer Company in 1984. Back then, Mr. Koch hand sold each account personally. As his company grew methodically on the east coast, he ultimately took the company national which is what the marketplace wanted.

Today, however, the market is even more crowded than back in 1984 and the beer quality much better. We can thank industry luminaries like Jim Koch, Fritz Maytag, Ken Grossman and Jack McAuliffe for creating the craft industry, but with that success has come a plethora of competitors.

The evolution of the craft beer industry has been one of sustained growth and expansion as consumers continue their foray into craft, graduating from domestic beer. Breweries that have been around for multiple decades are on the move either eastward or westward. Both Sierra Nevada and New Belgium Brewing have moved to the East. Lagunitas has expanded from Petaluma, California into Chicago. Green Flash is also looking to expand from San Diego to Virginia Beach. Many other regional brewers eye this freight-savings and freshness temptation. As some microbreweries evolve, they will be faced with a tough dilemma; stay put or expand to a second brewery site based on logistical efficiency and market share growth?

Most brewers will likely add brewing capacity rather than build a second brewery across country or simply increase facility barrelage by brewing more hours per day. Some of these brewers have reached the maturity stage of the product life cycle with their brands in their existing markets, thus the need to expand into new markets to keep their breweries at capacity and to justify these capital expenditures. Assuming favorable demand, this is an easy, but expensive way to gain market share. The danger of entering new markets through geographic expansion is that the market could be oversaturated (a likely scenario today) which may not justify this expensive and somewhat risky advance.

The warning here is you should be fully prepared before entering a new market. Just like Mr. Barowsky, you will need to do your homework and have adequate and dedicated personnel in place to sell the brand into the new market. As a firm continues to expand into new markets, resources can be quickly diluted then exploited by a larger competitor or by a local one that is solidly focused on the market you may be considering for entry.

As a brewer, distiller or vintner considering production expansion, especially in the craft industry, another review of the product life cycle is warranted. Ask your team if the brand is continuing to grow organically with strong distribution pull (i.e., repeat sales or shelf movement) OR is growth simply coming from the addition of new distribution, that is the opening of more states? Also, how are sales in your existing market(s)? Is more focus required here due to competitive threats? Do not forget your bread and butter. These are critical questions that need to be answered before the shovel breaks ground on a new facility.

As to the product life cycle, if your brand is entering the maturity stage of the cycle, it may not be prudent to invest a great deal into expansion, rather, you may want to look at upgrading the brand or trying some styles that are more reflective of market demand. I have seen this situation in San Francisco where consumer palates have turned towards high hopped IPAs at the expense of lighter ambers and pale ales. Brands that ignore these trends will soon fall by the wayside.

The United States is composed of many different markets each with its own taste preference profiles for food and drink. Never assume that what someone enjoys in San Francisco will be equally enjoyed by someone in North Dakota, Minnesota, Florida, San Diego, Oregon, Delaware or Chicago. Beverage marketers should adapt their brand strategy to the local market privations. National marketing plans for consumables that attempt to cover every US market are seldom successful. The companies that do this well are some of the world's very largest. These Fortune 500 firms have the expertise, experience, retailer relationships and resources to succeed on a national and international stage.

In an interview with Mr. Ken Grossman, founder of Sierra Nevada Brewing in Chico, California he cautioned, "...the days of starting a brewery, having the consumers pick and define a flagship and rallying your portfolio around this flagship and the national footprint are over. It would be very hard to do these days, very expensive. Just being relevant to so many different people in so many different types of geographies at a time when you cannot possibly 'out local the local guy.' We are in a fundamentally different growth model and industry than were even five years ago...[38]." I completely agree with Mr. Grossman, one of the craft industry founders and one its most successful. Rather than fantasize about national distribution, it might be more prudent for the small to medium-sized brewer to tailor his/her brand plan to the local demographic nuances.

Having studied hundreds of brands and consulted for dozens, I have seen companies over expand into markets unfamiliar to them and their products. A recipe for failure is the assumption that brand awareness is strong, that feet on the street will be made available when resources allow and that the existing marketing (including distributor sales incentive dollars) budget will stretch to cover the new territory(ies). If you cannot dedicate more sales people to the new geography and formulate a separate and substantial marketing "bucket" for the expansion, then given the added capital costs, the probability of success is curtailed. My question to you is: Do you really need to expand? That is, does there exist valid consumer demand for your products and beverage styles?

Marketing research will help answer this very expensive question via qualitative and quantitative research methodologies. If you are serious about expansion then research is imperative to improve your decision making and to reduce risk. The challenge today and tomorrow will be how to succeed in this exploding market with your brand. Expanding upon the market concentration strategy highlighted earlier in the Lestoil example, I now present to you a concept, fermenting in my mind for years, for your consideration.

"CASTLE KEEP"

Given the aforementioned forecasted expansion within the craft beer sector (aka, Skumeggedon), an appropriate survival and success option for small-medium brewers might just be what I call, "Castle Keep." This focused concept restricts distribution to a manageable geography or "selling perimeter" where brand awareness and sales pull are strongest amongst consumers, retailers, the On Premise and wholesalers. Under the castle keep theorem, the geography is adequately covered/defended by experienced brewer sales representatives who have cultivated long term relationships which continue to serve/support the brand franchise through seasonal and new product introductions. These relationships are the life blood of the brand and the brewery. Think of them as the supply lines to the castle. Under this premise, the brewery invests significant capital into a showcase tasting brew pub/tavern where new product focus groups are held, samplings performed and account buyers regularly invited for new product kick offs and entertaining. Think of this as the Castle's Inner Ward or "Bailey." The sales reps use the bailey often which reinforces the brand's local relevance and FRESHNESS.

Although not easily defined, the territory perimeter of the castle keep would be dictated by the brewery's distribution network reach AND by its On and Off Premise sales personnel coverage. Imagine your wholesalers/distributors as your knights on horseback. How far can the knights ride and still get back to the Keep by nightfall? Now think of your sales team as the archers – how far can they fire their arrows and still hit their targets accurately? Over extending either of these vital brand assets would certainly jeopardize the strategic foundation of the castle keep tenet. Imagine that the width of the Keep's moat directly reflects the relationships that your sales team and wholesaler reps have with local accounts. The wider the moat, the tougher it is for competitors to poach your handles or to take your Off Premise real estate. Conversely, the more narrow the relationship, or more shallow the moat, the easier it will be for competitive encroachment. Ask yourself, "how wide is your moat?"

The goal of the castle keep is for the brewery and brand to remain ingrained within the community fabric – thereby solidifying ties with loyal drinkers/supporters. This brand strength also acts as a deterrent, or "moat" to competitive brands searching desperately for new distribution territory. This competition may include a multi-national brewer or distant craft brewers seeking to expand volume through new real estate expansion. To guard against another craft popping up just around the corner, the castle keep strategy invests cumulative community chips to, "out local the locals" as Ken Grossman mentioned earlier[39].

Sierra Nevada has adopted an intriguing concept whereby they have built a tasting room/mini restaurant in Berkeley, California (they are based further northward in Chico, California) that brings a sort of "localness" down to Bay Area drinkers. The tasting room, coined, "the Torpedo Room" serves as a trial/sampling mechanism while positioning the brand as a local beer in the minds of Bay Area consumers. Sort of a, "hey we are local too, just a bit further up the road than some of the other brands you may be drinking."

Sierra Nevada uses the concept to also introduce some of their more obscure beers which helps maintain its craft/micro position within the savvy consumer mindset as he/she yearns to further discover new brews. The room is also offered to distributor sales reps that wish to invite their key accounts to come in and sample the fine collection of Sierra beers in a very tasting-friendly environment. From a marketing perspective, I see this as genius. If successful, I imagine competitors will follow suit on the concept. The Torpedo Room can also be considered as a competitive castle keep threat designed to research new market reception acting as a "research scout" for the mother ship brand.

If at some point, the brewery was performing at much higher sales levels than forecasted, then the perimeter might be extended. A second castle keep scenario might be researched at another geography, provided there was sufficient marketing research performed prior to this decision and resources made available to expand. Another option would be to erect a tasting bar similar to Sierra Nevada's Torpedo Room which in essence would serve as a market test for the brand in the geography under consideration. The castle keep formula is recommended for the small and medium to regional-sized breweries who will be vulnerable from attacks by large capacity brewers and upstart local Nano breweries.

With as many as four to five thousand breweries on the horizon, existing craft brewers will have to aggressively fight to maintain and defend precious market share, consumer relevance, wholesaler focus, sales volume, draft handle and retail real estate. Despite craft beer forecasts of 10% category share by 2016[40], the castle keep option is a potentially sound one for many beverage companies. Take it from Dick Yuengling, as stated from the film Beer Wars, his advice to craft brewers, "to grow slowly and methodically."

XV- MEMORABLE OFF PREMISE PRESENTATIONS & PREPARATION - Know and Appreciate Your Audience

Impactful presentations require hard work. I recall one that I had to make to the British media which included chairman level executives from British industry such as Marks and Spencer's, Tesco, etc. That day was unique in that I followed the presentation of an expert from the British food and beverage industry. The gentleman's presentation was mired in IRI data which began to put the audience to sleep. Worse yet, the presenter spoke to the audience in a condescending manner, putting them off all the more. The combined goal was to stimulate interest in his organization; Food from Britain; or mine: the Department of Trade and Industry.

I must admit that I had more than my fair share of butterflies in my stomach that morning. I am proud to say that I rehearsed this presentation (also out of fear of giving a lame presentation) over one hundred times either in front of a mirror or before colleagues. Each time I went through the presentation, I found ways to improve, to fine tune and to anticipate challenging questions. After getting up very early that morning and taking my run through the foggy, cold streets of London (where I almost got lost!), I psyched up for what was to be the greatest presentation of my career. Over the years I have found it valuable to arrive early for critical meetings where I may not know anyone in the audience. I make it a point to introduce myself to a few strangers and memorize their first names.

After the "famous" British food expert had finished his long-winded lecture, it was my turn. I proceeded to inform, educate and entertain the audience on the US food and beverage market while selling them (via the British Government Consulates) my two reports on such. In the presentation I worked in the first names of each of the people I met earlier. In one instance when I had a question, I asked "Bert" what the size of the US Scotch Whisky market was. Knowing in advance that he was in the business, he would not feel uncomfortable being put on the spot, especially after I had given him the answer while pouring him a cup of Assam tea that morning. Gathering names in advance makes for a more personable presentation, particularly when great emphasis needs to be made.

On several occasions when making a major point in the presentation I stepped into the audience, found that person, looked him in the eyes, used his name and made the point around voice inflection. This clearly won over the audience as I presented factually, personally and creatively. The rest of the presentation which included a personally filmed and edited US buyer video, proprietary Nielsen/IRI data, US Import data (that had not yet been publicly released) and much more, went splendidly.

After the presentation nearly 90% of the audience came up to my team's booth to purchase British Government services or to congratulate me on the presentation. My competitor sat stewing with a few industry colleagues glaring at me. The Chairman of Marks and Spencer's later wrote that my presentation was one of the best that he had ever seen in his career. The sales of my two industry reports also set international records for Her Majesty's Government. I share the above not to try to impress but to show via example how hard work, creativity and passion can help even the smallest winery, brewer, distillery and/or nonalcoholic manufacturer break through a sales audience's natural defenses, earn their respect and become their friend. After you have achieved this, you are on your way.

Taking That Expertise to the Chains

On the subject of getting key groups to want to sell and buy your brands, particularly for the smaller company with limited resources, I want to share another story that will be helpful. Tom Fox with CM Profit Group and Terry Lozoff with GY & K encouraged smaller beverage companies to use more objective data in retailer sales presentations[41]. I agree with this suggestion wholeheartedly, particularly for the large chains with the caveat that you don't exclusively rely on the data and simply forward it to the buyer. I have seen this done hundreds of times with little if any impact.

The way to win at the big retailer level is through "presentation synergy and tempered tenacity" (but do not forget my grandfather's adage which is equally weighted). For those of you who have never presented to "the Biggs" then this portion of my book is for you. Don't take this opportunity lightly as you may not get another chance. You will also need to be well rehearsed and suited up, yes, that means silk, wool and leather. My personal goal has always been to out dress my audience whenever I can, this in essence acts as a KDA for you and your company in the eyes of the large supermarket buyer and category manager(s). If you have never been on a headquarters call, then heed my advice.

Earlier in the book, I hinted at how bad things were between the bread company and their supermarket chain customer. I shared with you how I motivated the internal sales force; however, equally important was the need to shore up (actually reverse) relations with this largest retailer in the United States. To put the situation into perspective, this is just how bad it was:

> The buyer had completely thrown out the account executive (sales rep), not just from her four hundred stores but from the chain's headquarters. He was not allowed to present new items, discuss out of stock strategy, participate in upcoming chain schematic discussions or be included in store resets and grand openings. The results of the buyer mandate were catastrophic. Per IRI data, the bread company slid from the second largest brand in the west to a distant third.

> On every wave of resets the company lost further space as the market share leader and category captain further slashed Earthgrains shelf space and SKU counts. The leader also took incremental space at every reset and grand opening opting to devote such to their brands. New product authorizations made by the buyer in favor of the number one, two, four and five bakers escalated with profound effect on Earthgrains market share and revenue. Shareholders at Earthgrains demanded focus and results on this chain with the threat of installing new management.

After making my rounds to all the distributor locations and getting the route salespeople motivated, it was time to make amends with the retailer. But how does one climb up out of this cavernous hole? Rather than expect the buyer to see "the new guy" with open arms, I knew from researching the above issues that I would not even get through the (headquarters) door. So I started slowly, doing my homework. The route sales teams agreed to step up their service levels in our 4:30 am meetings and eliminate out of stocks. This was a top line concern with the chain buyer and her vice presidents. The route guys also agreed to improve their time window arrivals and shelf merchandising. This effort quickly showed dividends with the few remaining products that we still baked.

To increase my credibility with the drivers, I volunteered to ride with the busiest guys on their routes and "lump" bread. From presenting in a three piece suit at 4:30 am to getting into their trucks and helping make their delivery windows, my efforts became the talk of the water cooler. This was another first at the company. As I was walking back to the delivery truck about sun up to get another twenty-stack of fresh bread (a mobile rack that seems nearly ten feet tall and holds two pallets of bread left and right), a gentleman in a suit approached me to say hello. I introduced myself and gave him my card. It turned out that he was the area Division Manager with responsibility for fifty (or so) of the best-selling stores in the country! I gambled and asked if I could conduct a divisional (I made this up…) business review with on his stores' performance. He agreed so we set an appointment.

I returned to the office and started working on another presentation, although to a much different audience. In my meeting with the division manager (who was a Mustang guy) I absorbed a great deal by asking dozens of pre-prepared questions. As a result of the meeting, I learned that he conducts monthly meetings (similar to those held by the beer/wine/spirits distributors) but with the STORE MANAGERS within his division. So I asked if suppliers could make presentations to these managers. Pausing, he mentioned that the "big boys" often come in. Although not a small company, my employer was more than in the penalty box, which the DM knew about. I convinced him that it would be to his benefit to allow me to present if only for fifteen minutes. It took some convincing, including a lot of gearhead discussion, but he finally agreed and put me on the calendar!

The next month I arrived at one of the stores and was ushered into Customer Service then up a long stairway to the second floor of the store. I did not realize that the stores even had an upstairs! I then sat outside, patiently waiting my turn to present. I felt ready. I had my IRI, store by store data, focus group responses on some of our products as well as a ton of samples. It was 11:30. I sat there with my assistant until 12:15. The team from Pepsi went long and departed the room. The DM came out to tell me that we were up.

Finally it was our turn. We went into the medium-sized room and were almost knocked over by a heat/carbon dioxide tidal wave. The forty or so managers had been sitting through long, data-laden presentations since 7 am. The room capacity was probably more conducive to twenty, so managers were almost sitting on top of one another. I was baking like one of our loaves in my snappy wool suit but felt worse for my customers. As I began my presentation I quietly cursed the Pepsi, Coke and Dole guys for putting the managers to sleep. I tried to present my store data creatively but they were clearly burned out from numbers overload.

While presenting, I noticed that the managers looked hungry and sort of "presentation saturated." My upbeat nature and creative skills were not getting through. I wondered if they were hearing anything I was saying. I glanced over at the division manager who looked at his watch; I knew that we would not get another opportunity and just how dire the company situation was with this big league retailer. So rather than play focus group consumer sampling responses on our new breads, I took presentation synergy to a new level. Flipping to my best "good news" Power Point slide, I pulled the focus group compact disc from my boom box and dropped in a CD from my briefcase. I stopped the presentation at our most impressive IRI numbers and said, "You folks look like you have been through quite a few long presentations today. A lengthy pause ensued. "Is anybody hungry?" I asked.

At that point I had everyone's attention, including the all-powerful division manager. It was sooooo quiet. Some looked at me like I was a cup short of flour. I took my coat off and hit "Play" nudging the boom box volume. The room filled with goodness as, "I Feel Good" by James Brown echoed down the long hallway. The manager's initial reaction was shock but quickly turned to smiles. I instructed my assistant to begin tossing full sour dough loaves to the managers (pre sliced rounds), I tossed one to the DM. "This is our newest product, San Luis Sourdough, hand-baked right on the coast, fresh every day, from San Luis Obispo (California)" I bragged. We brought thirty loaves that day, just enough. To my surprise, a few of the managers got up and started dancing as we tossed full loaves to them.

That presentation/sampling story was shared by the DM back to the buyer that quickly led to a headquarters call. For the headquarters call I spent over fifty hours preparing the presentation which included data, forecasts, new items, video from our San Luis Sourdough bakery acquisition as well as edited focus group digitized clips, an out of stock strategy, special event sampling schedule and a revised delivery plan. I was able to reserve a private room at the retailer's headquarters much to the surprise of the buyer, which allowed me to prepare the room to my liking as well as rehearse in the new environment. This also set the tone of the meeting and the agenda which was run by me, not the retail buyer. Not long after the buyer headquarters call, Earthgrains received:

> -SEVEN initial newly authorized SKUs, over a dozen more were later authorized in over 400 stores

> -Reinstatement of more than five SKUs that had been discontinued by the category captain (the number one market share leader and a fierce competitor)

> -Reinstatement to the retailer headquarters for all "big brand" meetings on key topics at VP level and above

> -Appointment to the captain set team, a team that they had been banished from for over three years

-Approval to present semi-annual brand results to all division managers within the entire geography

-Invitation by the retailer to work with their category management team on company premises

-Retailer request for proprietary research report on potential for organic bread growth. This invitation was not extended to any of our competitors, just to me based on the analytics provided in our first meeting together and feedback from the district manager. I took the opportunity to share with the buyer future trend predictions that our company anticipated. This extra level of effort piqued the buyer's interest further.

Per IRI data, market share for Earthgrains doubled in just eighteen months after these meetings. I must also share that the first presentation to the buyer occurred on March 31st. Although I got no immediate authorizations from that meeting, the next day I thanked the buyer (via email) for her time and told her that our delivery team would be stocking the shelves (the entire Northern California division, their largest in the country) with ten new items that I had shown her the prior day. She immediately called me ready to blast then banish us forever when I told her that it was an April Fool's joke. She paused, then laughed. She then said that we could bring in seven new items for April 2nd – into her 400 stores...

The point is to know your audience and not be afraid to break out of the pack. In fact, for you to succeed in the alcohol business, given the limited real estate available and the tidal wave of competition, you will need to come up with highly creative presentations and methods to win over your crucial constituents OR you will be run over by your competitors.

Another example of "creative tenacity" comes from my beer experience with one of the nation's largest drug chains. For twenty years they refused to see anyone from our company at the district manager level. Even our president was rebuffed when he attempted to procure meetings. This chain was/is an integral part of this region's business being the largest chain in the area. So I set this chain aside as a matter of personal pride, "a gentleman's challenge or extra credit."

Over the course of nearly two years I collected tiny pieces of information on the chains' key personnel. I kept a note file and would pull it out at the end of the week in an attempt to connect the dots. There was not a lot there, but there was one key denominator. I learned that the two "heavyweight" district managers were "clothes horses." I heard that they liked to look "Wall Street." Several people that I interviewed during my research mentioned that one of the managers reminded them of the character Gordon Geko played by Michael Douglas in the famous film, Wall Street by Warner Bros.

Rather than send a box of cigars, I asked our company's owner if I could leverage his relationship with a very high end tie manufacturer and have several ties sent to the district manager's office. The request was approved. I included a note to each of the managers, asking for thirty minutes of their time and why it would be important for us to meet. The ties were hand delivered to their offices.

The next day, the senior manager took my call and granted me the presentation time. Since then, we have been the only distributor to present to this chain in our region. More recently, this relationship has blossomed even further. We took twenty-five of the chain's district, store managers and team leaders to three local breweries where we presented data on the craft business, trends, packages, style preferences and pricing. They also tasted many of our supplier's products. The end result was numerous authorizations, all at the expense of our competition.

Takeaways from that field trip are that retailers are thirsting to learn about the beverage industry. However, it takes extra effort to prepare a comprehensive presentation for a group like this. You must also first establish credibility and rapport with these contacts before you can offer to present to them.

The experiences above took years to achieve, but creative tenacity will oftentimes pay handsome dividends. This is the level of creative, "never say die" effort that is required for small to medium sized companies to succeed in today's sophisticated, expensive and hyper-competitive marketplace. Another point is that these challenges require a dedicated, roll-up-the sleeves, work ethic that I see in few workers today. There is no substitute for hard work. This, therefore, presents yet another opportunity for the upstart to get a foot in the door with a presentation on craft beer, how IPAs are taking over the region, what is happening on the Belgian-style front with sours, etc. You will need the right people who really thrive on these types of challenges and are willing to put in the effort. If you find them, you will be successful.

XVI- EXPLOIT YOUR PACKAGING

Chances are if you are reading this book you work for or own a small to medium-sized beverage company. Smaller firms have correspondingly smaller marketing budgets than the Fortune 1000 beverage giants. This means that the savvy entrepreneur or medium-sized company general manager must extract maximum results from limited resources. If you are a small to medium-sized brewer, an important part of your marketing is the product's package.

Craft consumers are often described as "promiscuous." A marketing executive's take on this description is that these consumers enjoy choice, novelty, brand discovery, quality, refreshment and a degree of hipness or coolness (i.e., image) about the craft brews or beverages that they purchase. If they really like your beer, they will become a brand ambassador for you. This is the sweet spot and goal for a small to medium-sized beverage company. Once you get that talk value, then you are on your way to building a consumer base that will generate enough volume for you to invest more marketing dollars in the brand's positioning. But you need them to remember and appreciate that package so that when they go into the store or their favorite bar, they recall your brand and make the conscious purchase decision.

If you review the extensive number of brands available in any given major metro, you will find some of the most creative and colorful beer labels and names that anyone could ever dream of. This is what makes the industry fun and represents your fishing hook for the consumer. This is not to say that a great label or unique beer name will guarantee sales success. On the contrary, the product inside must also be exceptional and consistent which is the reason for branding in the first place. Branding ensures that the consumer will come back to your franchise and purchase your products over and over again.

Attention Getting Beer Names – Bust (and remain) into the Black Box, Become, "The Evoked Set"

No matter where you are, you will be able to conjure up some really creative names that consumers will remember and tell their friends about. Keep in mind that nutty, creative names are fun but without some relevance or correlation back to your brand and brewery/distillery or vineyard, they will most likely be forgotten or confused by your end consumer. The savvy brewer, for example, will position his/her brand around a concept or theme, tying this back to the brand story. Take

Ballast Point, for example. All their beers relate to a fishing theme which contributes and RE-INVESTS equity into the brand positioning. As more consumers see these beers they become more familiar with the brand. This will increase the probability of purchase and loyalty to Ballast Point. This point is imperative to understand as the beverage landscape becomes more competitive. Here are a few excellent names that immediately stimulate interest which ultimately leads to trial. But do they relate to other SKUs in the brand family and do they reinforce the brand's position? Maybe, or maybe not.

Panty Peeler Tripel
Arrogant Bastard
What the Puck Pale Ale
Sod Buster Pale Ale
Possum Trot Brown Ale
Pigs Ass Porter
Coal Porter
Old Leghumper Porter
Morning Wood IPA
Homo Erectus
Homewrecker
Seriously Bad Elf
Bombs Away Double IPA
Custer's Last Ale
Hazed and Infused Pale Ale
Wanker's ESB
Bitch Creek ESB
Old Speckled Hen
Voodoo Bengal Pale Ale
EH! Canadian Style Ale
Wailing Wench
The Devil Made Me Do It
Bearpaw Brown
Small Craft Warning
Fiddler's Elbow
Butt Head
Moose Drool
Happy Ending Imperial Stout
The Dogfather
Wake Up Dead Russian Imperial Stout
Santa's Butt Porter
Git-R-Done Golden Lager
Fancy Lawnmower
Gone to Helles
Eulogy's Busty Blonde

Ex-Wife Extra Bitter
Alimony Ale
Loose Cannon IPA
Porkslap Pale Ale
Voodoo Donut Maple Bacon Ale
Buttface Amber Ale
Polygamy Porter
Trader Jose Premium Lager
Hoptimus Prime
Summer Hummer
Doggie Style Classic Pale Ale
Big Dick's Olde Ale
Bishop's Finger/Nun's Delight
Camel Toe Egyptian Pale Ale
The Men's Room Original Red
Faceplant
Panty Peeler
Collaboration Not Litigation
Tweason'ale
Homo Erectus
Happy Ending
Smooth Hoperator
Old Ringworm
Druid Fluid
Lumpy Gravy
Badonk-A-Dunkel
Nut Sack Ale
Icy Bay IPA
DD Blonde
May the Port Be With You
White Shade of Pale Ale
Vintage Horn Dog
Breaking Bud IPA
Hot for Teacher, Ms. Dopplebock
I'd Like to Buy the World a Kolsch
Jean-Claude Van Blonde
Thor's Hammer
Dirty Hippy
Drafty Kilt Scotch Ale
Old Scallywag
Block and Tackle Stout
Uncle Rusty
Marketing Ploy
The Dog's Hydrant (as opposed to the Cat's Meow) author original

Although you may not agree with some (or any) of my picks, the point is that choosing a creative name that relates to the brand family for your beverage line is a very important step in your initial marketing strategy. My recommendation is to name your beers around a creative theme or something to do with the brewery's origin and local geography, the area's history OR a passion that you and your brewers/vintners/distillers might share. You will see this in beers like Mendocino Brewing whereby all their beers are named after majestic birds of prey. One brewer names all his beers after dogs while another has each beer named after a World War II fighter aircraft.

Try to find a memorable and relevant common theme with which to differentiate the brand. This strategy, such as Ballast Point's (San Diego based) fish/sea theme, appeals immediately to people that fish, or might be fascinated by the sea or those that are attracted to the brand because of the colorful and creative art work. Or maybe they really dig San Diego! This suggestion does not guarantee an initial customer pool, but it certainly is a wise move towards capturing such.

Once you have selected the name(s) for your beers, you should hire an artist to create "the look" that conveys your perceptions and passion for the brand. This will be the first step towards branding your beverage AND will provide its first point of uniqueness. The graphic art should be colorful and creative so that it busts through the clutter already on the shelves and on bar draft handles. Be sure that your graphics team has a thorough understanding of competitive entries. It would also be wise to trademark these names and the artwork so that a competitor does not copy your efforts down the road. It is important to understand how critical packaging decisions and investments are to your brand's success.

If your brand look is dull or bland, the consumer will most likely opt for the more artful, exciting and/or creative selection on the shelf or at the bar. This creativity should transcend from the Off Premise to the On Premise; constantly re-enforcing that image in the mind of your soon-to-be-loyal customer. That means that you will need to duplicate the brand imagery onto your draft handles. Always remember that consumers are searching for something new and cool that they can share with their friends electronically so that that your "brand cool" makes them cool too, in the eyes of their social media network.

More Than Just a Name - Increasing Primary/Secondary Demand - for Craft Beer, a Win, Win, Win

Marketing purists generally define primary demand as consumer or buyer interest in a generic category, such as beer. Recall the 1994-2014 "Got Milk?" ad campaign for which celebrities donned white milky moustaches to support "generic" demand for dairy products? (According to the New York Daily News, the next campaign will be called Milk Life)[42]. If you look back at the ads you'll note that no brand names were ever mentioned. The campaign's goal was simply to increase American consumption of dairy products, namely milk. Increasing secondary demand means that the brand sponsor is investing in advertising or some form of promotional activity which will increase awareness and/or trial, thus leading to purchase intent, for that specific brand line.

Part of my job is to help fledgling craft brands grow and thrive in the hyper-competitive Bay Area marketplace (i.e., San Francisco). This wholesaler investment relates back to Product Life Cycle and Boston Consulting Group learnings. As you learn to understand these two marketing tools, you will appreciate why some wholesalers feel the need and offer the financial support for small brands that they anticipate will be medium to large brands in the near future. Savvy wholesalers know that the market is not static and that they need to continue to invest "in the bench" not knowing which brand will be the next Star. So they work hard on their smaller brands in anticipation and preparation for that next big player brand.

One of the campaigns I came up with that exploits smaller craft brand creative names, brand stories and logos while also piquing primary demand for local crafts is, "Drink California." The idea, which targets the Off Premise (Liquor and Neighborhood Store channel), is to promote California (local) crafts in a creative "Pavlovian" manner that also educates consumers as to where the brands come from. This in turn allows the buyer (consumer *and* retailer) to support his/her local brewers. In practicality it serves to promote both primary (drink California craft beer) and secondary (buy one of these local craft brands) demand. The beauty of the concept is that it provides the retailer with a key point of difference from the liquor store down the block.

As the campaign has evolved around holiday and sporting themes, consumers have begun to take notice of the ads and expand their purchase/sampling geography. "Oh I think I'll try a beer from San Diego this week," they might say or think in their minds, or without realizing, from their "black box." What is taking place in many of these accounts is what I call the establishment of "Venue Loyalty." By participating in the campaign, the retail account is investing in its own Key Differentiating Advantage.

When it comes to a venue, particularly an urban liquor store, there a few ways to build a KDA. Drink California is a successful one. I call this strategy a Win, Win, Win. The retailer wins over his/her nearby competition. The wholesaler wins because the account is taking on more of their craft brands. And the brewer is a winner because the retailer wants to carry the full complement of the wholesaler's local brands. This provides the shopper with more choice for native beers that they will become brand loyal to or will buy more of as they sample the offerings from around the state. This concept can easily be applied to other geographies.

Below are some examples of the campaign. You'll see how it has evolved from a Christmas holiday theme to football, basketball and now baseball. What I like even more about this concept is the minimal cost. All that was needed was some solid creative horsepower to jumpstart the idea around demand for local craft beer. The campaign is not generating meteoric-level results, however, retailers are actively requesting the next series from their wholesaler salesmen AND consumers are commenting on the creativity at the point of check-out where they are actively buying the brands promoted within the poster. This interaction with the retailer further builds Venue Loyalty as they return for more craft beer to that specific location. Below are some examples of the campaign and how it has continued to evolve.

THE CONCEPT HAS "LEGS" and CAN BE USED IN MULTIPLE GEOGRAPHIES

FOOTBALL SEASON and COLLEGE PLAY OFFS

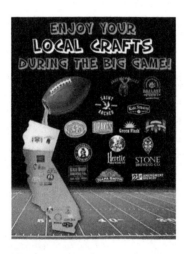

In the above creative, the headline was changed to, "Drink California" while directing the graphics team to further "Pavlovianize" (graphically) the great beer that is brewed within California. As you can see, the brewer logos also depict their local origin. My goal is to get potential consumers salivating for the local brands that the wholesaler and retailer carry.

BASKETBALL SEASON, the Campaign Evolves – Near March Madness with a new designer's touch on the Warriors' Splash Brothers and the team's incredible success.

BASEBALL SEASON – These were some creative concepts from the design team. This is a great example of how creative people can run with and expand a solid concept.

(Initial creative only)

As you can see, with a little creativity, these pieces are compelling and bring the curious consumer into the craft franchise while endorsing the local appeal. Another plus in favor of the concept is that the retailer will want to carry ALL the brands listed, which results in more points of distribution for the wholesaler and the brewers.

Taking It to the Biggs

The pieces you just reviewed will help the small to medium craft brewer get distribution via campaign inclusion. This may be a starting point in the brewer's introduction stage of the product life cycle. Once he/she gains approval in multiple "high-cred" liquor stores, they can objectively equate the store's sales velocity and use as a pitch tool to additional and larger accounts. As the battle for real estate continues to escalate, options like Drink California, might be a logical choice for the smaller brands.

When it comes to the ever evolving food and beverage industry, complacency is not a marketing strategy option. To further test the legs of my campaign, I decided to take it to the Biggs, that is, the largest supermarket retailer in the United States. This is where the small to medium brands will either succeed or be locked out, forcing them to claw for every inch of distribution in the smaller mom and pop liquor stores, delis or corner bistro "up and down the street" channel. That road has been travelled by many successful brands (study Jim Koch, for example) but it is truly an uphill, store-by-store battle made all the more difficult by the advent of so many new beverage brands. This following test example is critical for the fledgling brewer, distiller or vintner to study as mainstream brands dominate, block and defend limited cooler space in the huge supermarket chains. The left overs or scraps are warm sets and floor displays next to stale beef jerky.

Winning in the Biggs

Exploiting this large retailer's appetite for anything local, I realized the Drink California campaign would be right up the chain's wheel house. For this channel, commonly referred to as "the Chains," I opted to trim the campaign to a single brewer. With this focus on just one local brewery I then highlighted its brand story, featuring just a handful of the best products via some catchy copy. My hope is that the consumer will comprehend the Drink California concept, actively seeking out the brand featured on an end cap or floor display.

The strategy behind the campaign is that it allows the wholesaler to rotate brands through the concept, therefore controlling valuable real estate to the benefit of their portfolio while also providing a "KDA" for the mega retailer. The addition of the brand story takes the display level to an entirely new plateau not touched on by other wholesalers. Rather than build "case mountains" the Drink California display offers the consumer brand education which in turn leads to brand loyalty. This beer education is lacking in the category as consumers have no idea which IPA to buy or why. The beer market is similar now to that of the wine industry a decade ago when consumers had no clue which wine to purchase. Drink California provides that education that the consumer is lacking.

A significant learning from testing the Drink California concept was that the mega retailer's division management team was so interested in the campaign that they offered(!) to authorize select SKUs in the test stores, that were not in the master chain schematic. This is the crack in the door, the toe hold that high quality, small to medium sized brands must attack with all out tenacity. Approving SKUs out of schematic simply does not happen, unless you really have something special. By gaining even only a few stores of authorization for a fledgling brand that might not so much as obtain an appointment at the headquarters buyer level, could result in the "velocity cred" the brand so desperately needs.

It is ideas like Drink California that offer hope for the small brewer, distiller and/or vintner who realize that it will require strategy, creativity and tenacity to succeed in today's beverage industry, particularly at the big league level. Below is the actual field brand story written for Drake's Brewing along with several display pictures showing how the campaign looks in the stores. The campaign is directly responsible for getting more of Drake's SKUs into select stores which could lead to more authorizations.

Although not a great photo, how many store managers agree to pose next to a display? Here the store manager poses next to the Drink California display with a merchandising manager. Note the brand story affixed to the display on the right, second shelf down.

Below is the overhead banner used to attract consumers to the display and hopefully read the brand story. Note the use of Rate Beer data on the brand story and the overhead banner.

Although not the clearest of pictures, here is an exceptional real-world example of the Drink California concept in action. We got a COMPLETE end cap for the brand!!! This much more than I had expected. Plus, this was all incremental space for the brand, the wholesaler and...taken from the competition.

When it comes to real estate in the goliath chains, take whatever you can get. Here is a small store that received Drink California love. The overhead banner is double sided, so as consumers come into the store, that is the first thing they see upon entry. The store manager liked the concept so much that he offered a huge display area in another location of the store. That area will soon be devoted to Drink California crafts...

Another way to scratch into the Biggs is getting into a "bomber set." Here is a display negotiated between the US's largest retailer, at store level with the store manager, and the marketing manager of the wholesaler. Some of these SKUs are not authorized at the headquarters level. If they catch fire, the buyer will have to take notice and either give them more stores to sell in or even authorize, chain wide.

Exploiting the Art – Ninkasi & Lost Coast Brewing

Many craft beer brands, small batch spirits and boutique wineries' only marketing point of visual difference may be their labels and package. Exploiting this unique advantage should be done with great gusto. The more consumers and On and Off Premise buyers that are exposed to your brand marks the more familiar they will be with the brand and the higher the likelihood that they will try or request your splendid liquids.

A brand that I feel does this very well is Ninkasi, based in Bend, Oregon. Their strategy ties back to the Mesopotamian days where beer originated. "Ninkasi" was our first "beer god" and with the help of Lugal-Banda, successfully battled Zu, the bad guy god that stole away the tablet that held the first beer recipe[43]. To pay homage to her, the brand was introduced as Ninkasi and the beer styles all reflect back on this historic marketing treasure. This decision was a masterful stroke in the grand scheme of naming strategy.

Although not all the beers within the Ninkasi line follow through with the Mesopotamian theme, the graphics are exceptionally creative, colorful and memorable. The same can be said about Lost Coast Brewing's line. Their label designs are outstanding. The art work could be sold and probably do well in galleries. The point missed, however, is a common theme throughout the naming strategy. Here they miss the mark whereby they could have carried on the theme created by their downtown and alley cat styles. Although not easy to do, taking the extra step to weave the creative marketing theme throughout ALL the beverage styles (that is, the entire portfolio) to reflect back upon the umbrella brand, is a must for the craft/micro, batch distiller and boutique winery. As competition escalates, points like this should be adhered to in order to survive.

To further exploit this brand-art investment, the company should consider the merchandising of brand wearables that will serve to extend the brand message through the On Premise, consumer and distributor levels. If you really believe in your logo and the brand art, then invest in high quality wearables. Many small companies have tiny marketing budgets but usually can afford to purchase wearables. Having a "cool" line of "mini billboards" (shirts, for example) will be something that consumers will want to discover on your web site while they can be used at the wholesaler/distributor level as incentives and "thank you's" for over the top sales achievement. I have personally seen sales teams compete for wearables that are especially cool or retro.

If you opt to go with a low quality manufacturer, both the consumer and the distributor sales force will recognize these items as rags and treat them accordingly. I have seen boxes of unused, low quality wearables discarded by the wholesaler because they knew that the sales team would not appreciate or wear them. This results in precious wasted marketing dollars. Keep in mind that selecting low grade merchandise also reflects upon your brand position. Perhaps it would be better to wait until higher quality goods can be purchased in quantity by the fledgling beverage marketer or to sell the higher quality "mobile billboards" at the company's tasting room. As higher margin items are sold, economies of scale will afford a quantity purchase for select wholesaler sales teams.

On the topic of shirts, keep in mind that distributor special event teams love to wear cool (cotton) T and Sweatshirts at the special events where they work. This is another method of guerilla marketing whereby consumers will see your brand on the backs (and/or fronts) of the wholesaler special events crew who often work the entire event. While working these events I have been asked countless times where consumers can purchase these shirts. To that point, maybe the shirts could feature your web site and/or a hash tag for quick smart phone scanning. Extra T shirts (where legal) can also be handed to producer bartenders who will be serving your products at the festivals which results in additional exposure. Lastly, these shirts should be available for purchase at sponsored special events, this is yet another example of driving the marketing message down through the wholesale and consumer levels.

XVII- Guerilla MARKETING

As we all know, small to medium sized brewers typically do not have overflowing marketing budgets with which to promote their brands via conventional methods. For many of these brewers, guerilla marketing makes prudent business sense. Guerilla marketing basically refers to the sampling of potential consumers (recall "trial" from the Introduction stage of the Product Life Cycle) in creatively, unique ways. When given a high-octane creative boost, however, it becomes a results-driven marketing muscle plant. The primary goal of guerilla marketing is to participate in unique consumer exposure events that include targeted sampling opportunities and make a memorable, creative statement about the brand. Quality consumer sampling jump starts product trial while the venue contributes and reflects back upon brand positioning. Sampling also appeases the five senses. Let us now look at some Guerilla Marketing options.

Festivals – What a Perfect (and affordable) Opportunity for YOUR Brand

Trial, trial, trial equals buzz, buzz, buzz. Consumers need to taste your liquid and this element (especially within your Introduction stage marketing strategy) is imperative. If your product is as good as you think it is, then put it to the test. How? By having consumers and trade personnel try it. How do you get this exposure? Easy - hit the road. There are countless art and wine, blues & bar-b-que, farmer's markets, car shows/festivals and county fairs that take place throughout the year across the country. The trend now is beer festivals. City chambers of commerce and hundreds of non-profit groups are rabid to generate income from these exceptional "brand-trial" opportunities that allow you to interact with consumers who pay a significant entry fee for a four to five ounce beer glass to drink/sample all they want or they might get three to five tastes of
beer or wine or spirits for a nominal fee.

If all your small to medium-sized company can do is afford to attend and sample your products at these events, then this is where you **must** spend those limited resources. There is no better way to gain word of mouth recognition from the consumers who are discovering your brand than on their treasure hunt. Take this from a marketing guy with over twenty-five years of experience.

You know when your brand is a hit by the length and breadth of your booth lines as well as repeat interest. Think of these opportunities as "mobile focus groups." I have bartended many of these festivals and have witnessed consumers return as many as eight times to get more of the product we were serving. I noted that the booths to my left and right got little if any repeat customers. I urge you to attend these events and learn by observing consumers as they taste new and familiar brands. The beverages that they like will often receive social media play that multiplies old fashioned word of mouth exponentially by word of finger.

On that topic, with the advent of social media, you must/can now treat EVERY consumer/customer as a gatekeeper of your brand as each person has the power to introduce and influence dozens, hundreds and even thousands of friends (potential/future customers) to your company, brands and products. This potentially staggering power must be appreciated, respected and exploited to your advantage. How do you do this? Build a model (booth, impactful point of sale, etc.) for these beer fests and special events that reflects and represents your brand. Invest all that you can to make it look like your company and product line. It should attract consumers like a Star Trek tractor beam. You will know if it works very quickly.

Once you have your booth and look ready, cherry pick the individuals that will "man" the booth. These people must have the same passion level as you (try to work as many of these events as you can personally as the consumer interaction is invaluable) and know how to interact with people, know the important points about your line and be able to creatively inform potential new customers where to find the brands. Don't be satisfied giving potential customers a robot-delivered sample, make an impression, get to their "DNA Buying Bone!"

The more successful booths at these events typically have people that are especially out-going and fun. After all, if you can't have fun with beer, wine or spirits then you are most likely in the wrong business. Remember my grandfather's adage, "people buy from people they like." A final point on this critical recommendation is a suggestion to capture select consumers trying your product for the first time on video or still digital photography. You might even ask them a question or two, such as, "on a one to ten scale, how would you rate this product?" or, "Where would you like to see this product available in your area?" or simply, "What do you think about this beer?" You may end up with nothing but you just might end up with some gemstone clips that can be used to your brand's advantage on your web site, Facebook and/or made into presentations to retail and On Premise buyers.

With really enthusiastic responses, you could edit a brief video collection and use this as a presentation aid in your wholesaler sales team meetings to engage your internal customer and expose them to your brand DNA. As you can see, there is so much that you can wring from what seems like a simple beer fest. The vast majority of brewers, distillers and vintners that I observe miss this massive marketing gold mine. Put some effort and pre thought into it and it will pay handsome dividends. Buy a Go Pro and learn how to use this incredible marketing and sales tool.

This consumer interaction is the optimal time to share your brand story and generate "talk value" around your product line. You will be amazed to learn that many On Premise and Off Premise account buyers (including Chains!) will attend these festivals to learn about what is new and to just have some fun. Keep this in mind as you never know who you will be talking to. I recall pitching a client's brand at a blues and bar b que festival featuring over 300 craft beers and ciders. After a few minutes of small talk, the "consumer" identified himself as THE buyer for a large regional chain. I was blown away but realized the opportunity for my client so I invited him to sample all the products in a relaxed setting adjacent to our booth. He later authorized several of the SKUs as a result of this simple tasting and interaction!

Special Events

So you waited patiently in supplier line at your distributorship and finally you are in a major special event. Be it an art and wine festival, bar b que cook-off, muscle car show or blues/jazz fair, you will want to maximize this investment through guerilla marketing. Special events are perhaps THE best place for small to medium sized brands to spend their marketing budget. You can count on an event in a major metro just about every weekend. This represents exceptional brand trial opportunity for your growing portfolio. One word of caution, however, is the temptation to "mail it in" by telling your distributor or the event producer that your brand will participate but that there will be no one from the brand/supplier to attend.

Given the fact that there are multiple beer and wine festivals every weekend, the burn-out factor can be significant for your local rep(s). These valuable sales people typically are not compensated for their time "growing the brand." Initially they will participate in these events but with long work weeks and longer weekends to work these events, your reps will quickly say "yes" to the product donation and "yes" to the "will you need a volunteer(s)" at your booth question.

Having an "unmanned" booth at these events can oftentimes backfire for the brand. I have seen dozens of volunteers "work" a supplier's booth by oversampling themselves and not knowing anything about the brand. These are the kinds of events where consumers WANT to learn or ACTIVELY DISCOVER something new. Having a drunk or apathetic sampler at your booth may in fact turn consumers away from your brand, completely contradicting the effort/investment.

So what do you do? I suggest either compensating your rep, bringing in another employee from the company who can present the brand well OR hire an intern who might just be your next sales rep or brand manager. They will need to be over twenty-one in most states but training this intern on the salient brand points and retail (Off and On Premise) availability will further support this strongly recommended investment. As mentioned earlier, the savvy sales rep will also arrange On Premise promotions or features at several nearby bars after the festival has ended. This makes excellent business sense as the 21-35 year old consumer is just getting out of first gear once the festival has closed at five, six or seven pm. Keep that party going and in favor of YOUR brands.

Another reminder on special events, be "brand creative." There are so many ways to increase your brand's marketing presence at special events. Here is an example: Our company participated in the Bay Area's largest weekend jazz festival which brought just the right demographic exposure to our brands served at the event. We prepared all the price signage as usual which included ten by three foot banners, seventeen by twenty two inch, vertically-laminated booth pole signs as well as eight and one-half inch by eleven inch, horizontally-laminated table signage for quick brand selection and pricing communication. We then used "core buff" around the stage base to further promote the sponsoring brands. Lastly, we printed huge back stop banners that sat behind the bands at the rear of the stage. This would include non-alcoholic brand sponsors such as banks, supermarkets, etc. which resulted in some clutter.

So I got to thinking about ways to further differentiate our brands from those at this event, but in a more exclusively creative way. I came up with the idea of taking a sandwich board that we had dozens of (a sandwich board is a wooden triangulated piece that you will see placed on a sidewalk in front of an account displaying the specials of the day, typically announcing the happy hour brands and prices). Since we had so many extra sandwich boards I challenged our graphics team to design a background on a seventeen by twenty-two inch poster that incorporated the Jazz Festival's cool logo. I had the guys graphically wash/bleach this out a bit so that consumers could just make out the coolness factor from the festival's logo. We then made a master list of the bands appearing that day and what time they each played. Each of these posters was laminated for a classy gloss effect which made them sturdier. Behind the master band schedule was a poster for each band. Using "J hooks" from the local hardware store, I drilled out the sandwich board, which incidentally had perimeter branding for one of the participating breweries at the festival, and hung the band announcements on these hooks after hole punching each band's (17 x 22") poster.

Since we were the set up team for the beer, I had my team place these sandwich boards on the right side of the stage adjacent to the lead guitar player's spot. I then met with each stage manager prior to the festival opening and asked him/her to flip the "cards" as the next band began to play. This may not seem like a significant "big idea" but I must say that hundreds, if not thousands of consumers, line up to see which of their favorite bands are playing and at what time.

The actual band announcements, "Honey Bunny and the Big Guns" were so popular that some of the bands insisted on taking them home after their performances. Not all bands bothered with these, BUT, for those that did, the branding went with them to their practice studios and hung there as an additional reminder of just who sponsored the event and the brand got additional exposure from whoever gathered to listen at practice sessions. Total cost for this idea, $50 with printing and hard ware. We now erect the sandwich boards at all our events, at the special event producer's request.

Actual Sandwich Board used in field at special events – now insisted upon by event producers.

If You Do Not Like or Cannot Afford the Event – Then Start Your Own!

Anderson Valley Brewing Company, located in Boonville, California has slowly been growing over the past decade into a top fifty craft brewer. The Anderson Valley team is very passionate about their great brews and has created their own beer festival, held annually on a May weekend. Many other craft brewers are invited to bring their favorite brews and set up for the weekend. The event has become quite popular, selling out each year as craft-loving consumers flock to this tiny craft brewing hamlet in Northern California. Anderson Valley does not miss a beat with this creative investment by inviting select retail buyers and wholesaler sales people for "ambassador steeping." After one has experienced the brand in its own backyard, it is impossible not to be a fan for life. These types of events will take place more often in the future as other brewers realize the importance of a sizable tasting bar, exposure to the brand's DNA/essence and the brewery (with surrounding area) as a place for consumers, buyers and wholesalers to experience and interact with the brand.

On the topic of exposing key retailers to the brand's DNA. Keep in mind that many retailers, both On and Off Premise do not know as much as you do about the industry, trends, beer styles, consumer preferences, special event sponsorship community correlation, etc. I proved this point recently to myself when I invited twenty three buyers and regional district managers from one of the nation's largest drug chains to three local craft breweries. They jumped at the invitation and loved the experience. Throughout the day we answered dozens of questions about craft beer while they were able to learn how the beer was made and to converse with the actual brewers of such. The experience reminded me of a field trip but with much greater selling value. The chain has already increased their buying at store level for all three of the brands that they visited that day. The total cost split between the three breweries, $950 and lunch.

Please Come Inside

Another suggestion along the lines of Guerilla Marketing is the need for a customer-friendly tasting room. I have been to hundreds of brewery, distillery and winery headquarters which typically include tasting rooms. Some are elaborate and decadent venues. Other are simple rooms with outdoor awnings. I feel strongly that you have some "mother ship" location where consumers can identify with the brand's origin. At this location you MUST provide brand sampling for these prospective customers and GATEKEEPERS.

Appreciate and reward the sacrifice these people have made to take time out of their busy day to drive to your establishment. Most if not all of these people will share their experience with their friends and relatives via word of mouth OR through social media. You must appreciate and prepare for the influence that these people represent to your brand's success. Providing them with a positive and satisfying experience should be paramount, particularly if you are on a tight marketing budget. This requires the best customer service people that you have on your team. The potential that each visitor represents is enough for you to ensure that each and every person that comes to your location is treated accordingly. This red carpet attitude will pay dividends in the near future. To help visitors enjoy and share their discovery via Social Media, iSnap is a service that many beer and beverage companies are now using.

Having been to so many establishments, I was amazed at just how many were not appealing to enter and DID NOT represent the brand. The locations that were not "visitor friendly" seldom had a marketing department and were dictated by the owner who felt that investment in other parts of the company was far more valuable than "silly marketing." Many of those firms are out of business or are hopelessly caged in the Dog category of the Boston Consulting Matrix. The tasting room and point of entry for potential customers should be the "Brand Throne." This critical geography of the business should be a living brand extension of your company.

Potential consumers and trade buyers should be able to discover, touch, feel, smell, understand and embrace your brand DNA as soon as they set foot in this spot. The ambiance must reflect the brand personality, this is, where you invest to make the brand shine to convey its point of difference and to provide every visitor with a memory or "talk piece" once they have departed. You want them to share and experience their discovery with your story. More craft breweries are recognizing the marketing showpiece significance of their tasting room/headquarters. Experts at these details include Stone Brewing, Anchor Steam, New Belgium Brewing, Speakeasy, Guinness, Johnnie Walker, Jack Daniels, Silver Oak Winery and Ravenswood Winery.

> **Marketing Corollary #4:** *If your marketing budget is limited be sure to invest in your headquarters location so that future customers and retail account buyers will want to return to your brand through purchase and authorization. Think about this critical aspect to your business and how many times pictures will be taken on site and then shared through social media. This is one of the most important initial marketing investments that you can make. When designing the area, think about photo*

opportunities, angles and backdrops that will serve to further the brand image. The importance of sampling has been mentioned several times in this book and your tasting room is the perfect location for this to happen. Frankly, if potential customers can't try your product, the probability is that they will not buy or refer it to their network of friends. Do not scrimp on this important opportunity. A strategy should be devised for how the tasting room or front of your company should look and how it will be used to entice fledgling ambassadors to propel your brands. Make this your brand showcase and people will come there and bring their friends.

As the marketplace continues to get increasingly competitive, the smaller craft brands that cannot afford an expensive tasting room adjacent to or within their brewery might consider sharing a location with other nearby craft brewers, vintners and distillers. What I mean here is to build a series of tasting rooms in a touristy location that gets a lot of traffic and to share the costs with the other participating beverage companies. Think of the concept as "Craftville, USA." When marketed to your target audience, the tasting rooms become a destination point for consumers who will want to return again to sample, and discover, your beverages. I predict this concept to expand as so many brewers are popping up in major and regional metros but must invest the majority of their capital into the brewing process. If you invest in this idea then be sure that your staff is fully trained on YOUR brands.

It is imperative that you have a passionate ambassador representing your brands that can fully speak to the styles, the process, the packages (these should be displayed for easy Off Premise purchase) and "the story." Try to participate in the construction so that a good photo area is incorporated for social media photo exchange. And don't forget the power of music marketing at you respective location!

Shouldn't I Be Investing in Advertising?

The importance of trial, particularly during the introduction and growth stages of the Product Life Cycle, **cannot be over emphasized**. I recommend that you reserve as many events as possible generating an aggressive festival calendar that spans the entire year. Remember that you will only want to cover the geography that your distribution channel reaches. Go no further. Some marketers would disagree saying that you should invest your marketing budget in advertising to "get the word out." This is why it is so important to have someone on your team who understands what marketing elements go where, when and why.

As for expensive advertising campaigns during the intro stage of the Product Life Cycle, I recall a medium-sized beer supplier that had built a marketing plan around billboard and radio advertising. Although their brand was approaching the Growth stage of the PLC, I was able to convince them to channel their dollars back into samplings, which they did with solid success.

Once your brand has a solid footing in the Off and On Premise accounts that validate the brand's positioning AND it has been tasted by a reliable number of consumers, who now want to buy such, then you can begin to invest in the advertising side of the marketing equation. This strategy comes more into play in the latter end of the Growth Stage of the Product Life Cycle and has proven useful in attracting non craft beer users.

When I mention advertising, I do not necessarily mean "conventional advertising" such as billboards, magazines, television, etc. These vehicles may be inappropriate to your brand. If using conventional advertising, craft beer may lose authenticity with its consumer base. Television, however, works very well with image-driven spirits. A craft beer opting to use TV, might be perceived as a "big beer company." That could contradict most craft beer positioning strategies, so the media vehicles must be selected very carefully. Television might be more appropriate toward the latter stage of the Growth and beginning of the Maturity stage of a craft beer's life cycle.

Music Marketing*

The '60's -70's trend comes and goes but has some relevance with most consumers, particularly baby boomers who enjoy higher end alcoholic products. Younger generations also seem tolerant and accepting of this period. Motion picture and TV advertising agencies understand the passion and power of the period's music, even today. Numerous consumer product companies have used bands like the Stones, the Who, the Doors, Aerosmith, Led Zeppelin, and the Beatles to introduce their brands either on TV or via the 'Net. What does this have to do with the craft brewer? Please read on.

Consider Music Marketing (my own term) as a subset of guerilla marketing. Think of music marketing as your brand's sparkplug. Soul, funk and blues music have a way of transcending race and age barriers like no other genres of music. Soul, funk and blues music from the '60's – 70's is infectious and contagious. It gets to your "soul bone" which is connected to the "billfold bone." To exploit this concept, the craft beverage marketing manager should identify regional guerilla marketing events that are appropriate to the brand's target market and reflective of the brand's positioning.

There are most likely dozens if not hundreds of art and wine festivals (beer, wine, non-alcoholic beverages and spirits are often poured in volume here), chili cook offs, music festivals, car shows and county fairs held in your market areas. These events are targeted opportunities for brand sampling and selling. Moreover, festivals create a relaxed environment for subtle brand introductions. In the California Bay Area, there is an excellent event that targets the upscale beer and wine consumer. That event is the Walnut Creek Art and Wine Festival. This summer-time weekend event (held the first weekend in June in an area known as Heather Farms Park) attracts thousands of the Bay Area's highest income consumers and families.

Once your team has their target event list compiled the next step is to ask your distributor if they already service the producer of that event. If so, let them know that your brand would like to participate and be served there. Oftentimes these key festivals are locked up by the national brewers with extended contract agreements. Most companies might accept this response from their distributors and look for another, smaller fair. If you have done your homework and really want into a festival another angle might be to suggest a "micro/craft" tasting tent or booth. This is how smaller brands can be discovered at these larger festivals dominated by national beverage brands.

The distributor may or may not want to pitch this concept to the producer of the event as it means more work for them and often times the kegs or cases for these booths may be donated. If your distributor does not actively communicate with the special event producer, it would be to your benefit to contact the producer directly and meet with them to present this concept. The producer will most likely be interested as it will mean pure profit.

The best way to get them to say "yes" is to tell them that you will donate your draft or package beer for the right to be at this portion of the festival and in return the producer can charge ten dollars, for example, for three tastes of your micro/craft brands. This is an excellent example of guerilla marketing whereby your company avoids the high price of sponsorship and still gets a good location within a marquee festival or fair.

You should also be prepared in advance to request where you want that booth to be. Being too close to a stage can off-set the benefit of you or your team or the producer's trained (by you) servers being able to verbally pitch your brands to consumers AND invited key retailers due to the noise level. A popular location at these festivals is oftentimes adjacent to the muscle/classic car show that might be held within the overall festival. If the event does not hold such, then a suggestion to that effect could bring more patronage to the festival and thus deepen your relationship with this special event producer. The savvy marketer might even approach several of the local car clubs to see if they would be interested in participating. These "gearheads" are always looking for a way to show off their rides, and to help you sell your beverages.

On the music side, if you are successful in getting into these festivals, etc. then be sure to include music. As mentioned above, soul, funk and blues music harmonize together as an "audible tractor-beam" bringing in hundreds if not thousands into your brand essence. The trend towards these festivals/guerilla marketing is substantial as Fortune 100 consumer products companies are shifting their conventional ad dollars into these grass roots, "take it to the community" festivals. In the past few years, major special events with a long history are seeing participation from such mega brands and retailers as Safeway, FORD, General Motors, Sprint, Wells Fargo, Anderson Windows, Blackberry and many more. These companies, just a few years ago, would never have been seen at craft and art festivals. Now they have national travel teams like rock bands with multiple 53-foot tractor trailers that wind across the country stopping to set up at major festivals throughout the long summer season.

What does this mean for your brands? Additional trial and brand exposure as the Fortune 100 brands contribute by attracting even more consumers. On the downside, it also means that your booth will need to be that much more competitive to be noticed. I can recall an event that I attended on behalf of an artisan sour dough bread baker. This event featured hundreds of stellar craft beers as well as wines and gourmet food items. To break through and be noticed at this very crowded event, I set up a sound system and played '70's funk/soul music merchandised by a "Flour Power" theme.

To expand the theme, I hung eight track tapes and little smiley face balls from the booth for effect. We also hung a ten foot, full color banner Flour Power banner over the top of the booth. The music drew thousands of consumers to our booth which was poorly located away from the heart of the festival. Even so, we ended up as one of the busiest booths at the event! While they waited in line for our breads, consumers danced to the music all the while being exposed to our new items, brand logo and "brand essence." Our booth clearly became the most popular at the entire show and was surprisingly recognized as such by the event producers. To cross our "Ts" I also had the servers hand out coupons to buy the product at retail and prepped them for retail availability questions.

Another excellent opportunity at these festivals might be to team up with a condiments company such as bar b que sauce brand. By sharing the booth costs your brand can be the complement to the bar b que being served. Pursuing this route allows smaller firms to share in the costs of the sponsorship while allowing brand access and exposure to thousands of prospective consumers. Incidentally, consumers who love bar b que over index on craft beer and better beverage consumption. Another option would be to co-op with a winery or spirits company simply to share the costs of a ten by ten booth. This is less than optimal but better than sitting on the side lines at a significant special event. Be sure that you have adequate branding materials at these events.

You should also do your best to attend and be the one pouring your products. This consumer interaction/feedback is imperative for your success. It provides immediate product feedback that you can take back to your brewery, winery or distillery. It will surely impress your wholesaler, and you may even meet retail buyers from both the On and Off Premise who oftentimes have their guard down at these weekend events. I can't tell you how many times I have met key buyers at these festivals, sat them down and sampled them on the brands that I have represented. This "qualitative sampling" always leads to at least an appointment if not multiple authorizations at their chain, store or bar. Lastly, consumer research group, Mintel, found that 45% of consumers would try more craft beers if they knew more about them[44]. Keep this point in mind, but do not forget the music aspect which attracts consumers specifically to YOUR booth!

*Excerpts taken from author's article, *"Your Target Market has a Personality, Why Not Your Brand?"* published and copyrighted by the American Marketing Association, 8/13/2001.

Sponsorships – Why They Are Good and How You Can Get More Out of Them

Many large beverage companies get deeply involved with financially sponsoring major sporting events and concerts. This to me, a marketing guy, makes great sense. To the regional sales manager, it can lead to some pretty lengthy arguments over cost vs. sales benefit. "Sales" may try to dismiss brand sponsorship participation based on a sales volume (kegs) to dollar investment argument. In my opinion this argument is somewhat short-sighted as there are many brand benefits to sponsorship. Fortunately, "Marketing" will usually win this battle which is best for the brand.

On the subject sponsorships I need to share another "case history" with you. Back when I was the Brand Manager on the Honey Hill Farms Premium Frozen yogurt line, I had a small special events budget. As a fairly inexperienced Brand Manager, I figured that everyone would want to have our fine brand associated with their event. Then I learned the reality and the true cost of getting into major ("the Biggs") events. I could not just throw in the towel so I kept trying all the angles.

After getting laughed out of some producer offices, I met with the organizers of the Volvo tennis tournament in San Jose, California, now known as the SAP Open which is the second oldest on-going tennis tournament in the United States. I was able to get thirty minutes of time with the event producer, Mr. Barry MacKay a former tennis star and Bay Area native. As we got to talking, Mr. MacKay began to appreciate my enthusiasm and tenacity for the brand. The fact that I too was a Bay Area native and that we were an underdog brand when compared to a powerhouse like Haagen Dazs, (who were dragging their feet in negotiations with Mr. MacKay) helped my cause tremendously.

In our meeting he agreed to give tiny Honey Hill Farms, ice cream/yogurt category exclusivity, and multiple front section tickets for matches throughout the entire event, not one but two demo locations to sample consumers and distribute retail coupons, AND brand inclusion on all printed materials, scoreboard announcements and radio ad trailers for $5,000. Note that Haagen Dazs had been the sponsor for years prior to us getting that opportunity. This was HUGE for the brand from a positioning standpoint as the demographics skewed very upscale.

The facility itself was an excellent sampling venue for our target demographic. We could also leverage the sponsorship from an advertising perspective as well as a sales team selling tool. I immediately informed the vice president of sales after the agreement was consummated so that his team could tell local supermarket retailers that Honey Hill Farms was sponsoring the Volvo Tennis tournament. The results from this five thousand dollar investment included sales to the convention center, extensive brand exposure, public relations photo opportunities with the tennis stars and celebrities who we captured eating our product as well as entertaining key retailers in the seats that I had negotiated. This case history is brought to your attention, particularly to the smaller company owner/brewer/distiller, for you to realize that creative tenacity can pay off and with significant dividends. Even if you are just a little dog, you can still bark big. Later that year we overtook Haagen Dazs in two, key, West Coast markets per AC Nielsen data. That was a heck of celebration day for our little company.

XVIII- SOCIAL MEDIA – SO MANY OPTIONS

Wikipedia defines Social Media as, "interaction among people in which they create, share, and/or exchange information and ideas in virtual communities and networks. Furthermore, social media depend on mobile and web-based technologies to create highly interactive platforms through which individuals and communities share, co-create, discuss, and modify user-generated content. They introduce substantial and pervasive changes to communication between organizations, communities, and individuals." Social media differ from traditional/industrial media in many ways, including quality, reach, frequency, usability, immediacy, and permanence.

Regarding the interaction between the internet and social media, there are many effects that stem from internet usage. According to Nielsen, internet users continue to spend more time with social media sites than any other type of site. At the same time, the total time spent on social media in the U.S. across PC and mobile devices increased by 37 percent to 121 billion minutes in July 2012 compared to 88 billion minutes in July 2011[45].

In late 2013 it was announced that Americans now spend more time on the internet than watching their televisions. As an old school marketing guy, I view social media as a "marketing hors d'oeuvre." The hors d'oeuvre is an enticement or appeasement to find out what the main course is all about. Marketing's overall role is to build consumer chips of conviction towards a brand (or set the table) while the sales team is responsible for the close (get the buyer to say "yes"). Marketing, with the help of social media, gets the brand into the "red zone" while the sales team gets the buyer or the consumer into the end zone.

Here are some luminary comments taken from a 2013 interview with Dr. Philip Kotler on social media's marketing relevance. The interviewer was Mr. Niaz Uddin from eTalks[46]. *"The Internet is having an impact today that is comparable to what the world felt when Gutenberg introduced the idea of printing. The Internet, social media and new communication technologies are major game changers in marketing. No longer does the company own its brand by having a monopoly on communications about their brands* (this is so important to understand as consumers can influence your brand and sales with the swipe of a finger. Your goal is to convert them into brand ambassadors by the thousands). *It is the consumers and their peer-to-peer talk that is shaping our images of brands and what to buy and how much to pay. Furthermore, no company can afford to deceive customers without being quickly exposed on the Internet. The development of social media technologies such as Facebook, Twitter and YouTube are changing our tools for promotion."* There is much to be learned in Dr. Kotler's assessment.

One of the key take-a-ways is the immediacy that social media represents. Consumers that find your brand can, and often do, communicate this discovery to several, dozens and even hundreds of friends. Thus the reason to always tell the truth about your brands and to give these interested consumers updated newsworthy information on your brands. Many call this "telling the story." When crafting these stories keep in mind that Millennials value transparency which is a must in today's Social Media environment[47]. The pendulum can swing the other way as one bad brand experience can be immediately posted to hundreds of potential consumers via Twitter, Pinterest, email, blogs or Facebook. This is all the more reason to treat every consumer and prospective consumer as your most valuable asset. Think of them as your "field marketers."

Social Media is an affordable marketing tactic that puts the term "spreading by word of mouth" into hyper drive. I define it as a tactic because I don't feel that Social Media is a replacement for a comprehensive marketing strategy. Rather, I see it as a marketing plan adjunct, a piece to help attain much grander marketing objectives and strategy fulfillment. Also you must realize that Social Media is not directly responsible for sales.

A brand, product, person or company may have thousands upon thousands of "likes," but this is no guarantee of sales results, that is, six packs in the basket through the check out. Likes, (or site frequenting visits), and blogging about the virtues of how great your brand or product might be are all "marketing chips of influence" in your brand favor. They are contributory influencers towards the ultimate sale but do not serve as a substitute for going into the market place and presenting your brand to an off or on premise buyer. Today and tomorrow's consumers actively seek out and share their grass roots beverage experiences through Social Media. All you need to do is go to a busy craft bar and witness the value of "thumb chatter." Discovering a new beer or beverage earns the finder social stripes more commonly described as "likes."

As one amasses a keg full of likes, he or she in essence begins to brand themselves and becomes more socially relevant in the on line community. These participants then graduate to the level of credible expert on their field that they report on which earns them a social gatekeeper-like status with their readers/followers. The followers (friends) then subscribe to the gatekeeper's advice. These hard to find gatekeepers are certainly key people to influence with your social media brand stories.

You also want to get them to your tasting rooms, sponsored festivals, etc. Remember that the social media piece should be seen as a synergistic complement to a broader marketing plan and should not be relied upon as the focal point or primary investment of your brand marketing. To put it another way, social media is the invitation at your porch for prospective consumers to enter and then discover your brand. How social media is used and how the brand story is crafted, determines how many visitors you will have and, if they decide to stay. For very small firms, social media will be a predominant part of the marketing play, however, it is my experience that sampling, particularly in the introduction and growth stages of the product life cycle should take precedence over any other investment of time or money.

Ideas

Conveying your company's passion can be done via Social Media. Consumers are hungry to learn about your brands and the DNA behind them. One idea to capture such is to get a high quality digital camera, perhaps a Go Pro Hero, to tape your next brewer sales presentation, beer festival, food pairing, tap take over or retailer grand opening. Learn how to edit the digital tape and then place short relevant segments or clips on your brand's web site and Facebook pages. Consumers will love to discover these interesting points about your team and brands while you can direct trade buyers to the sites for interesting and unique points about your products, which will contribute towards authorization. The edited sessions can also be used by your sales reps as well as the wholesaler teams who might use the material on a lap top or iPad during their account presentations. On this topic, Craft Business News reported that ABC Fine Wine and Spirits is employing a "Beer Consultants" program in more than 30 of their 140 stores. The "beer geeks" will educate consumers on craft beer, styles, pairing, etc., AND will make recommendations.

How valuable would it be to have a social media piece available on your web site or Facebook page or even downloaded into these beer consultant's iPads for immediate viewing at the consumer point of purchase? This is just another example of how you can leverage or "synergize" storytelling and brand fact video coverage with social media to generate sales results and educate/raise brand awareness with potential consumers. As I think about it, how powerful would Twitter be for your company if "ABC Fine Wine" was featuring your craft beer line or a new varietal at their stores? Your team's Twitter efforts would help drive more consumers to this retailer which would place your company in higher graces with the retailer.

Other ways to use social media, provided it is legal in your state, is to announce pub crawls in the cities and neighborhoods where they are conducted. Perhaps your brand has a mascot which could be followed, via Twitter, from account to account? Anderson Valley Brewing does this successfully with their mascot, Barkley, the "bear/deer," while Nesquik does something similar with their bunny at many public events and wholesaler sales meetings. Your sales rep could make this a fun evening via creative twitter feed while generating more consumer participation in the pub crawl. The results could then be shown the following week, for example, to the participating accounts which might lead to more authorizations. This takes little effort and costs nothing, you just need some creativity and the passion to execute it and then use it to generate more sales.

With the advent of seasonal beers has come the "seasonal seasonal" as I refer to it. More commonly called the "Brew master or Limited Brewer Series, etc." I understand the rationale for expanding a brewer's line and the marketing benefit gained by brewing somewhat obscure (but cool) beers. The challenge, however, is for your wholesalers to get these sold, along with all your other SKUs and their other supplier's products as well. What can happen is these second seasonals can stack up in the warehouse which signals to a forecasting manager that they are slow moving items. This is not the perception/reputation you want at your distributor/wholesaler. One way to avoid this backlog is via Social Media. I have seen brand managers and supplier sales reps successfully "pre sell" these limited edition, quick-hitting beers by sending a teaser email or Twitter announcement to buyers informing them of the limited availability, the description and the allocation. This email could also be posted on a web site or Facebook page which are good tools to pre sell the scarcity of these limited edition beers. If done correctly, they will be sold out before they are even brewed, much to the delight of your wholesaler and your brew master.

Early in the book I mentioned some findings from Bump Williams, an expert on the beverage alcohol industry. In a 2014 interview with Beer Business Daily he voiced a majority concern now held by today's supermarket retailers (or bar owners as well) that, "when it comes to beer brand loyalty, they (retailers) see it eroding at a very rapid pace[48]." He went on to describe how brand loyalty is dying due in part to so many new beer introductions resulting in process overload and price and package confusion. The Millennial is also psychographically categorized as brand promiscuous by packaged goods marketers. With so many options, how could you blame today's beer consumer who oftentimes is simply looking to buy what's new. Bump classified this shopper as, "I haven't tried that brand yet."

These findings should be very concerning to you and your marketing department. Why? Because after finally winning the battle to get into a major supermarket, will your brand really have a chance to succeed given the nature of today's flighty craft beer consumer? This is of course not to say that there are no brand loyal consumers, just ask the folks at Sierra Nevada, Anchor Steam, Sam Adams, Dogfish Head, etc.

So what can you do to protect your brand and get it rocketing towards the growth stage of its product life cycle now that you have gained some supermarket and distribution success? Use social media as CREATIVELY as possible to foster consumer interaction. Your team must make a connection, as many as possible, with your consumers.

Get out to the beer festivals and talk to every person there, perhaps you use music to touch their soul bone (as a memorable KDA) so that when they walk down that beer aisle or open the cooler door, they remember how your brand touched them. Get involved with the community, participate in charitable (and high profile) donations, engrain your brand into the community, and then communicate all of this, as well as your unique story via social media. Did you know that in May 2013 there were 1.25 million Google searches for craft beer? (Source: Wikipedia). This curiosity was driven by Craft Beer Week promotion and hype, but think about what just a few percentage points of that total could do for your brand.

Here is a simple example of something I did for a brewer relating to social media. I used my relationship with a major chamber of commerce who was looking to add value to their quarterly business exchange/networking functions held for their members. So I got a craft beer interested in donating some cases of beer which I personally sampled at the event. For the craft brewer's small product donation their brand logo was included on the chamber's web site which receives as many as one million hits per month(!) and they were included in all email blasts announcing the event to the chamber's 10,000 or so membership.

The evening of the event, I sampled about 150 white collar middle managers who quickly learned and became fans of the craft brand. Pictures were taken of them consuming the beer and then placed on the chamber's web site. Many of the attendees took "selfies" of themselves with the unique brand (I placed some custom point of sale banners near the sampling table anticipating photo opportunities) and then posted the pictures to their favorite social media platforms. This is just a taste of how social media can be leveraged to your brand's marketing and selling benefit all at very little cost.

I do not profess to be a Social Media expert but do see its usefulness in assisting with the delivery of the marketing plan. It certainly is a quickly evolving and growing tool. On the topic, be careful not to hold social media responsible for Return On Investment (ROI). Think of Social Media as your electronic kid on the "cyber-corner" dancing with his big pointer billboard, inviting prospective customers to come experience your brand. There are many companies that can help you in designing a successful social media approach. There also some solid companies that can help you measure your results.

Some social media options to consider are Pinterest, Twitter, web site linkage, Rate Beer, Instagram, Tumblr, Onion.com, Foursquare, Gawker.com, Reddit, Verve, Fanfare Mobile, iSnap, Flickr, news-blogging, Linked In groups and industry individuals, Facebook, beer festival live digital brand responses, special events that can be used to your social media advantage as well as tasting room branded photo backdrops.

Also try to find "local" media sites such as Bold Italic (relating to the Bay Area in Northern, California) that specialize in "happenings" in local markets that might just be within your distribution scope. Keep an eye out for apps that will allow consumers to buy beers for their buddies and dates at their favorite bars by sending them a pre-paid drink to their I phone. The recipient will simply show the drink (on their phone) to the bartender who will get it for them. This tool will be useful to the savvy craft brewer who looks to recruit bars that wish to exploit this technology.

What is imperative for your marketing plan is to erect a social media foundation/infrastructure to exploit so that you can be ready to share newsworthy events, experiences, stories, successes, new products, opportunities and updates on a daily, weekly and monthly basis. This social media "platform" should be able to traverse across all your marketing tools, further embellishing the ever precious Four Ps (marketing mix). The key will be to stay on top of what works for your brand and what you can afford, but make sure that you are constantly getting quality brand interaction and contact from your multiple audiences. Engagement and participation are vital steps towards a sale and ultimately, brand loyalty.

A warning on social media; be sure to check with your state's alcohol laws and how your actions on social media might be portrayed as adding something of value to a retailer. For example, in California, under ABC law, a brewer can't "like" a retailer that sells their beer there. Under California ABC law, this is considered a thing of value that helps to sell alcohol and is not allowed so be sure to check your local state laws before you go crazy recommending and liking accounts.

XIX- SELECTING MARKETING TALENT & ETHICS

I vividly recall a meeting I was invited to at a Northern California transit agency. I had no idea what the meeting was about but knew it had to be important as there were thirty-forty chairs at the massive executive conference table/runway. A strange feeling came over me when I noticed all the play toys, spongy rubber objects and piles of candy at each setting. I sat down at the head of the conference table opposite the company's general manger. In strolled about thirty employees ranging from a part-time receptionist and full-time union drivers to scheduling engineers and the general manager who was also an attorney.

The group then began eating their candies and playing with the toys placed in front of them. I was dumbfounded, watching quietly and wondering how much money was being spent or lost on this expensive team's play time. "How much is the agency spending per hour right now?" I thought to myself. After fifteen minutes the general manager asked for attention. We were already a half hour past the scheduled meeting time. She then announced that we would be developing a tag line (slogan) for the transit agency as "we" begin writing the marketing plan. Interestingly, this agency had never had a marketing plan in its history.

The general manager then went around the table soliciting ideas from each of the attendees. She also asked us to define marketing in our own words. My jaw dropped in disbelief. "Somebody wake me up from this day mare!," I thought. When she got to me she introduced me as the agency's marketing consultant. "Mark, how do you define marketing and what slogan can you put into the bucket?" She actually had a bucket that people wrote down their "marketing" ideas on a piece of paper to be placed inside like you would at the Colombo Club raffle. The submitted ideas were to be voted on afterwards by the group, after the candy ran out, I guess.

I informed the team who I was and my background trying to be diplomatic as I strangled a blue, furry, rubber ball. Scarfing down another candy bar, the rotund general manager looked to quickly move to the person to my right. Retaining the floor, I stood up to state that I would not require any marketing ideas from the group. The general manager choked on her fifth Almond Joy spitting up some dried coconut. I cited an example from the scheduling department, explaining that I don't go to them to suggest how to set up the routing system nor do I get on the bus to tell the drivers how to drive (glancing at the drivers at the table playing with their Slinkys). I thanked them for their interest and assured them that my team would have a complete marketing plan, with tag line in so many months. I got up and left the group to finish off their candy. The look on their faces was memorable. Fifteen years later, the agency continues to use the plan I prepared for them. What a fine opportunity for a 60 Minutes segment...

The point here is not my lack of diplomacy (I was younger then) rather the importance of finding a true marketer for your brands. Brewers, distillers, and vintners all know how to make and take great pride in the liquids that they create. The error sometimes made by these people is they overestimate their skills thinking that they can do just about anything, including being a marketing expert. With nearly three decades of experience, I have learned that people that commit their lives to a specific field of expertise such as brewing beer, engineering bridges, distilling whisky are the ones that should be doing these tasks. They have the most expertise, education, creativity and passion for what they do and should be regarded as the credible source for such. This is their specialty, their life's calling, it's in their DNA. This credo also applies to marketing specialists. There are very few Bo Jacksons running around corporate America.

I am advocating that you spend the time to find a truly creative marketing person or team that can expand upon and execute the strategies and ideas that you are reading about in this book. You, the reader, are probably too connected to your company and brands to even see the marketing options that are right in front of you. What you need is a creative marketing person or team that can sit back and look at your business and brands objectively to better see the creative options. If you can't afford a full time marketing person then don't rely on the people that answer your phones, that pour hops into the boiler tank or your over inflated ego for ad hoc ideas. Hire a consultant or ad agency who has credible references and expertise IN YOUR area of business. Marketing can't be taken for granted or ignored in today's crowded beverage field. This is so true now more than ever as competition escalates to new highs in the US beverage market. I suggest taking another look at the book's front cover. J.B. Shireman, former Vice President of Sales and Marketing with New Belgium Brewing said that "brewers should be prepared to invest much more against marketing and branding than ever before due to an impending beer fallout[49]."

Also do not assume that you have your marketing base covered because you hired an MBA to execute your marketing. Spend a great deal of time on this hire, find out what classes they actually took (how many were marketing?), what projects or internships they worked on and if they have some advertising agency experience. I have met many people in my career that claim to be in the marketing field but in reality have little creative ability (and may have never even studied the subject!) which in my opinion you are born with. This creative bent is what drives that type of person to marketing and advertising as a high school and college student. The result can be just the person or consultant that your brand needs. That person or consultant should LOVE the beverage alcohol business and see it as fun and one of the most creative outlets for their passion, all of which your brand will benefit from. Or, you can conduct a roundtable with all your employees but don't forget the Almond Joys!

Ethics - White vs. Black Hat

As you enter larger more sophisticated markets with an expanding team, you will soon learn that many accounts require "something extra" for placement consideration. This is a decision that you should make prior to entering the marketplace and a discussion that you should have with your wholesaler partner prior to visiting any account. In many accounts your only "greeting" will be, "what's the deal?" This gets frustrating, repetitious at times, and downright irritating when you see some of the brands that accounts carry instead of yours because your competitors opt to, "pay to play." Typical deals will be buy "x" kegs and receive "y" (typically one keg) for free. A typical account deal might be to buy five kegs and get one free. Although illegal in most, if not all states, this deal can get even richer for the greedy account. The question is, "will you pay to play?"

Some brewers are absolutely refuse to "donate" free product, run a credit card scan or provide free sporting tickets for pourage rights. In certain parts of California, some brewer/distributor partners will build entire draft systems in return for the account's promise to pour their brands. Other accounts demand, and get quarterly payments of as much as five hundred to one thousand dollars per handle. I have even heard of suppliers paying $10,000 per handle in some west coast markets, $30,000 for two! This handle rental/lease "payment" is illegal and expensive and usually agreed to in an undocumented handshake agreement. In light of these pay to play options, I suggest the best tactic is to discuss what accounts make sense for your brand with your wholesaler partners and be prepared for some outrageous and spendy requests.

I have observed a brand from San Diego that refuses to compensate an account for carrying their beer. This policy has not hurt their sales whatsoever as the brand continues to sky rocket in all markets where sold. This brewer's tactic is to provide the account with data that shows their brand's profitability against a much lesser known or inferior quality brand that might be on tap only because it was dramatically discounted to the account, i.e., "paid for." Their consistent reluctance to pay to play might result in some missed opportunities but it actually works to their benefit as the brand does best via selective distribution. Selling beverages with a no black hat policy will require more homework so that you can show the retailer the increase in turns over inferior liquids and the benefit to his/her check totals as well as the image/positioning advantage conveyed by carrying your brand in his/her establishment.

XX- EXPORTING & IMPORTING – WORTH THE TROUBLE?

The once very healthy Import beer category is now being inadvertently repositioned by the craft segment. Import drinkers are trading laterally to bigger tasting crafts after recent price increases from some of the heavyweight imports. High-end Belgian style beers are white hot - especially sours - and command the upper tier price points with seemingly inelastic ease. Conversely, mainstream imports are scrambling to entice domestic premium beer drinkers to their franchise. This desperation move is an attempt to stem market share declines through packaging duplication. Despite the category achieving nearly 28 million bbl. in 2013, high share import brands have been busy introducing a plethora of "me too, domestic-like" packages designed to appeal to the domestic beer drinker. These package classes, once a unique sanctuary reserved for American lagers, are now targets by several imports.

To take share from domestics, the large import brands have introduced eighteen pack cases, three packs, long neck six packs (Heineken has introduced a long neck), twenty four pack loose cases, and five liter fridge mini kegs, all mimicking domestic premium brands and their loyal blue collar consumers. What impact does this have on these brands in the minds of better quality beer consumers?

Import beer price points remain competitive in an effort to lure the domestic beer consumer while craft brands tap into once loyal, white collar import drinkers. To maintain these price discounts, many "import" brands are scrambling to remain competitive by brewing either domestically or in Canada in an effort to curtail freight costs. In this cost cutting strategy many of these brands are now appearing with great regularity in bargain basement retailers. These are stores where the brands would never have been found only a few years earlier in their product life cycle. Unfortunately, this tactic is appropriate for brands entering the Decline stage.

What are the consequences to these once great import brands? What does a consumer think about the brand equity and quality when they habitually see these once powerhouse brews in the depot-like stores in their neighborhood? Distribution, packaging and pricing decisions, as mentioned above, do not bode well for these once heavyweight titans. As a brand continues to dance towards the commodity freeway, there will be no way back to that once coveted super premium positioning. Some brands will be fine as the demographics of the US continue to evolve but

European imports, other than the white-hot Belgians - will need to make some critical decisions for the long term health of their brands or risk falling into the "Dog" box of the Boston Consulting Group model, or worse...

The bright spot on the import side are the Belgian higher end beers which the market can't seem to get enough of. In many retail markets across the country Belgian style beers are gaining space from wines and beer brands, but not craft. Belgian imports have grown at an annual compound growth rate of 33% since 2000 while Belgium moved into the fourth position in top beer exporters to the US behind number three, Canada. Constellation Brands' Modelo Especial is also on fire surpassing Corona Extra US sales for the first time in history[50].

On the export side of the equation, the Brewers Association reported craft beer export volume increased 36% over 2013 to 383,422 barrels. Canada was the number one importer of US craft beer up 93% (up 140% in 2012), at 130,000 bbls while Sweden was number two at 44,000 bbls, up15.5%. The United Kingdom brought in 8% of US craft brews followed by Australia with 5% and Japan with 3%. A total of just eight countries accounted for 77.4% of all craft exports in 2013. Growing demand from within the Asia-Pacific area is expected to increase, especially from Thailand, Singapore and Hong Kong[51].

As craft curiosity and demand continue to grow around the world, US brewers should consider export opportunities. On that subject, a savvy brewer should inquire to their wholesalers if they sell to ship chandleries which can generate additional case sales while exposing the brand to international markets and consumers. It is also suggested that US craft brewers contact the US consulates oftentimes located in the countries that they are looking to export to. The offices may be staffed with commercial officers who can help expedite the export process to that country and might offer support for "joint ventures" to the country during a prominent food and beverage show whereby the prospective craft exporter can test the waters at a government-subsidized booth within the trade show. The commercial officer might also be able to generate a list of distributors and importers located within the target country for email, phone or personal presentation. Having worked in the British Consular Corp for seven years, I sent many a US exporter in that direction.

XXI- EPILOGUE - FADS, TRENDS and IDEAS to WATCH FOR

One idea relevant to small to medium-sized brewers, vintners and/or distillers is the concept of teaming together to build a sampling location featuring multiple small and local brands under one roof OR it could be multiple tasting rooms in an adjacent area. Picture it as "Beerville" whereby consumers drive to this location to sample (and discover) new beverages. Law compliance would be imperative but the concept helps the smaller brands to gain trial while they could all share in the combined costs. Trendy mobile food vans could be invited to make this a "destination" particularly with social media pre planning.

To make the venue even more worthwhile to attend, a muscle car show could be added or a blues band every weekend. The combined brands would then share resources to promote the venue to drive consumers to the sampling location. I have seen this concept work quite successfully in the wine industry for small, fledgling wineries. There is no reason that it could not be applicable to an organized craft beer or spirits guild, for example.

"Power in Numbers, Stepping Backwards to Step Forward"

On the topic of pairing, I see a similar trend towards centuries-old European food faires (picture 17th century Florence, Rome, Dusseldorf, Cardiff, or Kerry) whereby "cheese mongers" will offer their local dairy collection along with local bakeries, butchers, artisanal distillers, vintners, florists, fish mongers, and others. This concept, although rare in its infancy, is actively underway in Walnut Creek, California. The idea has taken root based on farmers' market popularity. The target audience demands local, organic, fresh, healthy and flavorful consumables and for years have supported the ever-expanding farmers market there. This support is the marketing research behind the step backwards in time.

The food faire concept is precisely the place to be for craft beers, especially those just beginning. Those needing that precious toe hold. As food faires sprout and flourish in US metros, participating brands will benefit through association/participation. Retail buyers (Off and On Premise) will take notice of these artisan, old-European food & drink hamlets, frequenting them to learn what the next trends and "in" brands will be. Look upon the farmer's market as the "hamlet incubator." Although, hard, piece-meal work, this will be a legitimate avenue to pursue for introductory stage craft beer and spirits brands. The key will be to identify which farmer's markets have enough patronage, consumer loyalty and local government foresight and support to merit the next step.

More Trends

Although not an idea, a trend coming our way will be large company (Fortune 500) acquisitions of craft breweries or just their brands. I am not referring to the obvious beverage companies, rather the largest of consumer packaged goods firms and even others who recognize the growth and profit potential from acquiring top tier crafts. These acquisitions will be simple ways to buy more shelf space and control smaller brands. They may also pave the way for new distribution not experienced before as they learn the beverage wholesaler ropes. Do you know where all your common shares are?

Another big company trend coming is Starbucks rolling out with alcohol sales. Already in test, Starbucks will sell alcohol through thousands of select stores over the next several years[52]. This effort will include beer. Keep in mind the Starbucks customer and how he/she parallels the craft beer target profile. This might be worth a trip to Seattle considering the fact that they have 11,500 US locations. This expanding point of purchase trend is already being successfully seen in the powerhouse Whole Foods chain which sells draft beer and just hired their own brew master to begin brewing custom beers exclusive to Whole Foods. Beer no longer is only available in just liquor stores and the corner bar, it looks to be nearly as pervasive as soft drinks. Will vending machines be next once ID scanning is perfected?

An interesting occurrence at a large supermarket retailer is their test to infuse additional flavors and spices into branded craft beers via a coffee press configuration. The thinking behind this is that the retailer will have their own version of the branded beer style available everywhere else, thus providing them with a KDA. I am not extremely comfortable with this given the definition of branding and must warn craft brewers to find out if their beers are being modified in any way. If so, I would suggest there be an agreement to ensure quality control as it relates back to the brand and the equity invested within.

Distribution has gone from many to an industry consolidation and back to specialty distributors who can bring retailers those little known brands of beer, spring water, spirits and/or wine. Watch for more of these specialty account distributors to flourish in major metros as the large wholesalers take on too many SKUs resulting in diluted service levels and account prioritizing. The large wholesalers therefore, will be forced to trim bloated portfolios, shedding poorly performing brands or cutting back on second seasonal programs. This step towards logistical efficiency may open the door further for the entrepreneurial specialist distributor who will be looking for upstart brands and may be willing to take on some of the large wholesaler discards. To offset this reality, some of the very large distributors are introducing specialty/craft divisions that focus on the small to medium sized crafts therefore giving them more attention and allowing them to incubate within these "craft cradles" until ready to be spun into the mainstream wholesaler model.

By 2020, there will be just 650 distributors left in the US[53]. If you currently have some success with self-distribution I strongly suggest maintaining these relationships long after you appoint full time distributors. I recommend this because you will be able to use these accounts to sell in your highly unique beers which can be a bane to the large, space-strapped wholesalers. The trendy, one-off and/or seasonal within seasonal beers, however, contribute towards the brand's unique personality and help to differentiate it from the many competitors in the marketplace. These long-time, loyal accounts might also serve as test markets for new styles from your brewery. So really scrutinize this decision before severing ties in favor of geographic expansion.

Today it seems that consumers have a near frenzy for local beers, spirits, wine and beverages. In the food industry the "farm to table" concept has gained solid ground with consumers and buyers. This local or grassroots appeal derives from a yearning for connection and bonding which serves to shun and distance these drinkers from the likes of the multi-national brewer. The giant brewer's response to this trend has been to introduce "zip code" beers designed by their brew masters within each of their US-wide breweries. Local also means fresh and "neighborly" in consumer minds.

Promiscuity, as mentioned earlier in this book, however, is rampant within the craft sector as beer drinkers continue to crave more from brewer flavors, styles and variations. Look for craft companies to reinvent their line ups with India Pale Lagers, cider/ale/lager/spirit hybrids, beers aged in spirit casks, beer cocktails, hoppy-hefes, shandies, new yeast strains, infusions and sparkling ales or lagers. This will be the way into the market for some smaller brewers who can chisel into the beverage granite wall with highly unique niche offerings.

Beverage Synergy – A + B = C

Synergy is defined as the addition of two distinctly separate parts, that when combined - result in a third sum, that is much greater than the two individual portions left alone. I have noted in my career how often we miss the really big picture in our daily business lives. What I mean by this is that we seldom have the time to step back and review how we could combine relationships and "business elements" into a much greater return for our effort. Some examples of "Mark's synergy" follow.

When I first started working in the beer distribution business I wanted to "get on base" with my employer so I, like most business people, leveraged prior relationships from previous positions. In my prior appointment with the British Consulate I had come to appreciate the monthly networking mixers that the British conducted at various bars throughout San Francisco. As a beer distributor, I realized that by bringing in a large drinking group to a bar could result in some dividends for my employer and several of our suppliers. So I contacted my former colleagues and found out what criteria they used for venue selection. The monthly groups ranged in size from fifty to two hundred depending upon the time of year and the venue. As for venue selection criteria, the only things they wanted were space, proximity to work and quality draft beer. They were not influenced by happy hour discounts.

As I got to know more about this group I convinced them to let me select the venue. Having a group of over one hundred very thirsty drinkers in your back pocket was quite influential as far as my selection of the final venue. In this case, I picked a British style hotel that was also a draft non-buy (non-buy means that the account did not buy any of our draft beer) for the company. As I began bringing the group to the account another consular group decided to join (the Australian Consulate) who was occasionally joined by the New Zealand Consulate. As the groups got larger so did the appreciation of the General Manager at the account. This appreciation led to two draft handles for our brands at the expense of our competition. Since the relationship was so strong I also negotiated a discounted room rate for all company and supplier employees which is still in effect and has been so for over ten years. This is an introductory example of how I define business synergy.

The prior example is one in which the fledging brewer, distiller or vintner could attempt to implement. In fact, the three could even partner in this concept. The take away here is that many suppliers quickly give up on pursuing a market by stating a myriad of excuses such, "oh there is just too much competition in that market, or the competitors are too large, we don't have a chance." I have heard these excuses many times and so will you. Think about how I brought together several key groups to the mutual advantage of my employer and the beer supplier that we represented. This idea certainly makes the most sense in a major metro area. A place like southern Bakersfield most likely does not have an international consular corps, there but I bet they have a busy Chamber of Commerce.

These groups make it a habit to meet either every month or quarterly. All you have to do is find out who the right contacts are and then begin working with them. This might even be your first customer, for a brand new product, which could lead to many more authorizations all because you would not accept the excuse that the marketplace was too difficult to penetrate. I find the art of creativity severely lacking today which leads to opportunity for those that possess a "never say die" level of creative tenacity.

To be certain that you understand the term positioning and how vital it is to your brand's success, here is an example of "positioning synergy" which I find absolutely brilliant. In 2014 there was just one international superbike race held in the United States. The race took place at Laguna Seca raceway in Monterey, California. Italian super bike manufacturer Ducati teamed with Italian super premium sparkling water brand San Pellegrino and reserved a large portion of seating for their best customers and trade contacts. Peroni also got involved via the local beer distributor.

This positioning synergy resulted in the elevation of all three brands to an even higher level within the target audiences' mind. This is perhaps the best example in this book of how beverage brands leveraged an event to further propel their image up the positioning ladder. San Pellegrino also took advantage of this opportunity by conducting wholesaler incentive contests in other markets for sales teams to compete to attend this grand event. Distribution increases were significant while retail account entertaining resulted in greater supermarket displays and relationship building.

Sponsoring an exclusive super bike race may be nowhere on your marketing radar, however, note how Peroni got in simply by asking their wholesaler to sell the brand into the concessionaire who the wholesaler had long term relationships with. This is something that you can request of your wholesaler and need to watch for throughout the year. There are many high and medium level car races that take place across the United States, all of which attract many consumers. What is the most popular spectator sport in the US? Auto racing. How brand relevant would it be for your brand to be sold at one of these venues, particularly if you had, "GT-500 Stout" or Racer 5 IPA? Maybe the answer comes back "no." Do you pout and go away? No, you ask if you can sample your product at the venue and if you can donate some product for full profit sales in return for a sampling booth. That just might get you a meeting with the concessionaire. From there it will be up to your skillful selling. As you have seen throughout this book, I have had some success making things happen simply by asking and being persistent. When on a tight budget, keep these learnings in mind and remember that often the squeaky wheel gets the attention from your wholesaler.

Another example of simply using creativity in a synergistic way involved an On Premise customer who was building out a quick order food and beer venue in their very large parking lot as an extension of the mother ship restaurant. They came to me requesting a draft beer line up. Rather than rattle off a basic list of beers, all that would be pervasively available to consumers in this hyper busy tourist area within San Francisco, I came up with the concept of offering them just California craft beers and to promote such via a California map showing where each beer was brewed. This concept exploited both the interest in local beers ("A") as well as meteoric demand for craft beers in Northern California ("B").

The result, a novelty that tourists appreciated and could return to, to try other beers from local breweries. It also gave this account a Key Differentiating Advantage that its local competitors could not easily match. This is now a place for consumers and tourists to go discover great, local, craft beer and one that they will make as a destination point ("C"). The end result is that this wholesaler has ALL the draft handles at this venue all due in part to some creative synergy.

Another trend is the formal organization of "Influencers." These are people that have thousands of social media followers who are invited to meet at a major metro Chamber of Commerce or high end hotels to discuss current and future trends. In San Francisco for example, these networking meetings are taking place. I describe them as sort of a social media fusion. For small to medium-sized brewers, it would behoove them to have a relationship with the organizers of such meetings. While conducting the networking session, products are sampled so that these key influencers can discover them, then share with their legion of followers. This is what I have done for some small brands. The cost is minimal while the possibility of gaining significant awareness substantial. Keep this in the back of your mind as you enter major metros who typically have professional and well organized chambers.

To add synergy to the recent San Francisco experience, I asked the Influencer meeting organizer to direct the group to one of our largest On Premise accounts. I predicted they would inquire about eating venues so I asked my contact to direct them to this excellent restaurant venue. This forethought was appreciated by the account's general manager which serves to deepen our relationship with the account.

On the topic of Influencers, in relation to Guerilla Marketing, do not forget to tip your favorite coffee barista with a bomber or six pack of your beer. These people are go-to gatekeepers in the millennial beverage-advice hierarchy. I have done this and know that it helps create and spread "brand buzz."

Review of Key Points

- Understand the definition of Marketing; to determine legitimate wants and needs for a product or service and satisfy such with your product. Marketing is delivering that "need satisfaction" to your pre-defined Target Audience and the strategy behind the manipulation of the "Four P's": Product, Price, Promotion & Place (Distribution) throughout the brand's Product Life Cycle (Introduction, Growth, Maturity, and Decline).

- Define your KDA – Key Differentiating Advantage. This is not always easy to do. The business owner must think about what truly makes his/her product unique or different from that of the competition. An example would be: "Lake Tahoe Golden Ale the only craft beer brewed with Lake Tahoe blue water." Once you have this then use it in all future materials and presentations. Cumulative Repetition!

- Once you have your product ready to go, the next step is to build your distribution footprint. This is priority before promotion, advertising, etc. People need to be able to buy your product then you can tell them about it.

- If your marketing budget is tight then invest in Trial especially in the Introduction/Growth stages of the PLC. Trial is the best way to get your product into the mouths of your target audience. There are so many sampling opportunities today which include beer festivals, art and wine fairs, bar b que & blues weekend events, car shows, etc. These events represent the perfect venue to generate trial and awareness for your new product. Keep in mind that consumers enjoy going to these events and typically have their "buying guards down", opting to look for or discover new things. Don't forget to have your brand story polished and ready for all to view.

- When you get the opportunity to present your brand to a key account buyer, be well prepared. This means generating a professional presentation that best represents your brand and company (quality-wise). This presentation also gives you the opportunity to exploit your brand's KDA via creativity, research (know the market and the retailer in advance) and passion level. Try to "out present" your competition with a unique, well-rehearsed and creative presentation that will make an impactful and memorable impression.

XXII- CLOSING

Thank you for reading this book. I hope that it will instill or inspire marketing learnings within you and spur creative thinking. As beverage professionals we all compete for share of stomach but should try to work together collectively for the betterment of each of our categories. I also want to state that I mean no disrespect to any of the companies that I refer to in this book. I tried to give you my perspective on how we got to where we are and fully appreciate and marvel at both the marketing and economies of scale achieved by the goliath brewers and consumer packaged goods companies. Intra-industry finger pointing, however, will only serve to open the door further for products that might take share from the entire category. You craft guys and gals should appreciate the distribution infrastructure that has been created over the past century. Without such, the cost of market entry and distribution would be prohibitive. Let's be respectful to those that built this great delivery system so that we all can enjoy and flourish from it.

We aren't "vendors" "suppliers" "reps" or "wholesalers," we are all people; so let's treat each other that way. Without suppliers, vendors, brewers, wholesalers, brokers, importers, supermarkets, drug stores, retailers, bars & nightclubs and distributors, we wouldn't have an industry and we wouldn't have jobs. To think of it another way; who is more important the rock star or the fan? Without both there would be neither. I want to leave you with an important quote from one of our top marketing minds in the country. This is a final question posed to Dr. Philip Kotler from a recent interview.

Why do you think marketing is a great tool to change the world?

Philip Kotler: "Marketing's starting point is with consumer well-being. Marketing is about the maximization of consumer well-being. It also takes into account the well-being of employees, distributors, suppliers, investors and other stakeholders[54]."

I have told you repeatedly that the retail and On Premise battle will not be easy. But do not let anyone sway you from your dreams. Remember my grandfather's sagely summary from thirty years of field selling, "people buy from the people they like." My contribution, as a Colburn, to this is that everyone has a different button, all you have to do is learn (strategically probe) where it is and push it. This is a fun business, so go enjoy it! May you and your family have a long, healthy and happy life time.

And remember that the beer can does not fall far from the trailer...cheers.

iii-APPENDIX

The following distributor survey is used to provide wholesaler management with critical input on a potential new brand. The instrument's objective is to ascertain existing distributor response and results to the brand relative to the enquiring wholesaler's interest in authorizing the product. This survey is included to provide the small to medium beverage company with some insight as to how some wholesalers evaluate new brands prior to authorizing them and some of the steps they take in that decision process.

SURVEY

1-What made you decide to authorize brand X into your distributorship?

2-How long have you carried the brand?

3-Please comment on repeat order frequency:

    3a-Average cases sold per month? Current sales per month?

    3b-Average case growth per month?

    3c-How many cases do you expect to sell in 2015?

4-Please profile the consumer that is buying this product?

5-Where are you having the most success with this product, - On premise, Off premise, Supermarkets, mom and pops (Indies), Drug, C-Store...?

6-How has your relationship with supplier of brand X been?

7-Has the supplier kept to their promises?

8-How does the supplier of brand X support their brand? (Mktg materials, etc.)

8a-Does the supplier co-op their incentives or are these 100% them?

8b-Does the supplier co-op their sales support materials (i.e., permanent POS) or are these 100% them?

8c-How does the company handle slotting fees (where legal)?

8d-Sample policy?

8e-Who pays for ads? Is this 100% them or 50/50 co-op?

8f-Do they pay their bill backs promptly?

9-Do they have people in your market?

9a-How often do they work the market?

10-Do they have people calling on the Chains & C-Stores?

11-What is your opinion of their team, are they well managed?

12-Have you executed any incentives on the brand? Results?

13-Are they reasonable regarding distribution & sales goal expectations?

14-What is the Trade's feedback on the line?

15-What are consumers saying?

16-On a 1-5 basis, how satisfied are you with this brand in your House? (1 very dissatisfied – 5 very satisfied)

17-Any other comments?

INTERVIEW WITH BOSTON BEER FOUNDER/BREWER, Mr. Jim Koch

The following questions were posed to Jim Koch on a visit he made out to a San Francisco beer wholesaler.

1-Given the proliferation of craft/micro beers in markets across the United States and the expected opening of at least another 700 micro breweries in 2012, what trends do you see on the craft/micro horizon?

> *There will certainly be growth as the home brewer popularity graduates to the level of small brewer. We estimate that craft beer will account for a 10% share of the market by 2016. We anticipate the blurring of "zip code" breweries that operate in reduced geographies.*

2-What will it take to win shelf space Off Premise and to capture some draft handles On Premise, given the craft/micro proliferation?

> *Brewers will have to earn their shelf space. They will have to brew unique and delicious beers – not just by bringing out another IPA. Craft brewers need to have beers that are truly relevant based on consumer wants and needs. Don't just change the color of your sheets.*

3-Will shelf space come at the expense of domestics? Of imports?

> *I hope not. I would prefer to see space come from wine, soft drinks and bottled water. There is no benefit by taking each other's share. We need to work together (brewers) on ways to engage drinkers – in new and interesting ways to try craft beer.*

4-From your traditional brand building experience at Boston Beer Company, how significant do you think Social Media's role will be in the growth of the micro/craft industry?

> *It will become increasingly important for craft brands but it won't change conventional marketing strategy (or replace it) as people still watch television, listen to the radio and read magazines.*

5-Are you seeing traditional marketing budgets shifting to more guerilla marketing investment in the beer industry?

> *Craft brewers use whatever means they have to reach their drinking public(s). They also can't use mass media like the domestic brewers do.*

6-Is Boston Beer Company shifting towards guerilla marketing?

> *Our people emphasize education with our consumer audience, our retailers and our wait staff partners while we increase availability through distribution. We focus on selling to bars and their customers.*

7-If you were starting Boston Beer Company all over today, what would you do differently than you did back in 1984?

> *I would not have any investors.*

8-What is the next hot beer style coming our way?

Cider.

Mark Colburn outside Fort Mason pavilion (San Francisco, CA) with Jim Koch, Founder of Boston Beer Company.

INTERVIEW WITH DOGFISH HEAD FOUNDER/BREWER and Chairman of the Brewer's Association, Mr. Sam Calagione

The following questions were posed to Sam Calagione on a visit he made to a large craft distributor on the West Coast.

1-What is Dogfish Head's new product decision process?

> *I look for niches that don't exist. I analyze the wine, food, art and music world for clues and cues. When I find something we brew a tiny batch of it at the brew pub. We then see how it sells and may take it to a beer fest and/or build some social media buzz around it.*

2-What craft beer trends or styles do you see in the next five years?

> *Millennial want less sweet and more sour or bitter as evidenced by the popularity in IPAs and sour style beers. They also want choice with little loyalty. Brewers will need to maintain quality control. If they don't millenials will broadcast their negative experiences over the Internet much to the demise of these brewers.*

3-How do you decide on what SKUs or brands to discontinue?

> *We don't kill any, we just hiatus them. Our top ten brands from the last ten years – continue to grow. We remain humble and continue to tell a strong story.*

4-What is your opinion on the canning of craft beer? On plastic kegs?

I am OK with cans. Our culinary angle better suits bottles. The European plastic kegs seem to be ok.

5-What do you see as the best method to market craft beers?

Use events (special) and social media. These authentic marketing moments can be captured and shared through social media. I am jaded by television – the old fashioned yelling at consumers.

INTERVIEW WITH Bev Mo! BEER BUYER, AMY GUTIERREZ

1-How long have you worked for Beverages and More?

I have been with BevMo! for 18 years and the Beer Buyer for 7 years.

2-What do you see as the current craft beer trends?

The hottest trends right now in the craft beer industry are Collaboration beers between breweries, session beers, ciders and barrel aged beers.

3-What advice do you have for small to medium sized craft brewers?

The advice that I have for a small to medium sized craft brewery is to start with a good solid business plan upon roll out of your new brewery. If the brewery is already established, make sure you have a solid plan to roll out a new beer. Be ready to do business electronically. Understand that if you cannot keep in stock at current accounts, don't roll out more.

4-What are your selection criteria and expectations when evaluating a new beer?

In my selection process I look at the hottest trends in the market by brewery and/or by style, take into consideration what our customers are requesting by local market and also by store space and by category. The expectations are that we have all the proper paper work filled out and turned in to us in a timely manner to be first to market. We need to make sure that the product is set up in the right stores for maximum turns and freshness.

5-What do you expect a beer supplier to do as far as support once BevMo! has taken on their product?

I expect a beer supplier to educate their distributors on how to sell a new brand and/or style, so they can in turn educate our associates on how to sell to customers. I expect them to offer us programming and solutions to help advertise new product; whether it be in store, email communication, our web site or their own marketing plan.

6-What do you see as the future of craft beer?

The future of the craft beer industry right now has unlimited potential. With all of the new breweries being opened and existing ones expanding, the competition is more competitive than in past years. Consumers are being trained to try new brands and exciting new flavor styles.

7-What do you see as the future of imported beers?

The future of import beers will continue to evolve with advertising and newness, as the competition grows within the craft segment. We use the imports as profitable traffic drivers to build continued business. This business is driven by a handful of products; we are trying to expand the reach to consumers to expand their taste and trial of different packages, like what is done in the craft business.

8-Of domestics?

The domestic business is trending negatively, but not a category to be forgotten. We are continuing to find ways to maintain relevance and stay profitable.

9-Where is BevMo! as a retailer? Any major changes coming?

As a retailer beer is continuing to trend up. Over 3 years ago, we tested warm shelf, style set schematics in a few of our existing California stores, and since have rolled that concept out in all of our new 2.0 sets, we started with Washington State, and all 10 stores there are set in this manner, plus all new stores that have opened since WA state and we just remodeled all Sacramento stores to reflect this change.

10-Will BevMo! increase their beer sampling program, that is, in more participating stores?

In all 151 BevMo! Stores, we have a license to do in-store tastings.

11-Do you feel that the sampling program is a success?

I feel that our sampling program has been a success in the past and will continue to evolve with our new partnership with Greenhouse, as our tasting partners. This is a great service we offer our customers and we are excited about the new partnership, as they will do all of the scheduling, measure sales and educate their staff on the products being tasted, and in turn educate our customers.

CRAFT BEER – Matter of Semantics or a Sustainable Key Differentiating Advantage?

There has been significant press/blogging/tweeting/bar discussion concerning who and what constitutes a true craft beer? This issue has been brought front and center by the Brewers Association. The fact of the matter is that the multi-national factory brewers, such as ABI, know where the growth will be coming from in the next decade and plan to dominate the craft category. As stated earlier, this will make the road a much more difficult for the small to medium-sized brewer to succeed. Some argue that consumers are being deceived or duped by the multinational factory brewers with "crafty" brands like Shock Top. It may appear deceptive to position a brand as a micro/craft and conveniently omit the parent company of manufacture. It is equally deceiving to fabricate a limited liability corporation with a "crafty" nameplate in an effort to hide behind the "mother ship." This tactic has angered a percentage of traditional US craft brewers.

Does the consumer really care? Perhaps; then again perhaps not. An intriguing point was made in the Nestor vs, Diogenes debate on the topic in Craft Brew News where Nestor explained that, "we categorize beers by what they are, not by who makes them[48]." His logic therefore is that brewer designation or size is not the evaluation criteria used by the consumer, rather the purchase decision should be made on the nature of the beer. This logic is obviously up to the consumer to decide.

I recently was at bar b que where I was given a pint of Blue Moon served with an orange slice. I must say the beer tasted exceptional, like a craft. My best buddy has since shifted from being a loyal Pyramid Brewing

Hefeweizen drinker to drinking Blue Moon and does not mind that it is owned by MillerCoors. Now he can get his twelve-packs at just about every retailer across the country. I am also friends with home brewers that have stepped up the ladder to retail direct store distribution. They are upset with the multi-national factory brewer tactics and I empathize with them. How can the small to medium brewer react to these moves? Although not the answer, here is a possible tool.

The craft governing body, for example, the Brewers Association should develop a list of qualifying criteria that would establish those brewer's as "Artisan Craft Brewers." This designation, which amplifies Mr. Nestor's idea of Real Craft Beer, while excluding the multi-national factory brewers from what Mr. Diogenes characterized as, "masquerading craft brewers[55]" could include a national logo which would serve as a subtle key differentiating advantage for all brewers that met and continue to meet the artisan requirements. Possible qualifying criteria might consist of all or a portion of the following:

1-Brewery is independently owned
2-Barrellage is no greater than 300,000 barrels
3-Entrepreneurial owners possess the majority of the company's stock
4-Brand is distributed regionally, that is, it is not a fifty-state distributed brand
5-The Company has no more than two breweries in the US
6-The brewer employs no greater than five hundred employees
7-The brewery does not participate in scan back retail rebate programs
8-The brewery does not participate in On Premise tactics which include free kegs or rebate programs
9-Brewery will not ship direct to retailers or their warehouse systems
10-Members brew only using a set/list of authentic brewing standards (governing body to define these)
11-The brewery is in no way or part affiliated or owned by a much larger corporation and is not defined as an LLC, sub chapter corporation or strategic business unit of a much larger parent
12-The brewery only ships fresh beer (unfrozen) and maintains beer that is kept cold and fresh until it reaches its final retail location

The above is just a start and needs refinement but the concept is worth studying and debating. Finally, a possible tag line that would support the brand mark on all packaging and kegs: "Be True to Your Craft."

Marketing Brief, Brand Overview and Scorecard

These tools can assist the beverage supplier or brewer to better understand and communicate their business to their wholesaler partners. I created these forms for brand managers to complete with their supplier partners which have multiple uses.

MARKETING BRIEF

BRAND/SUPPLIER:	
2016 Actual Cases vs. 2016 Projection:	
% Up or Down over 2015 (est.)	
2016 Annual Forecast & % +/- over 2015:	
Brand's KDA (Key Differentiating Advantage):	
Key Holidays &/or Beer Selling Occasions:	
STRATEGY for ACHIEVING 2016 PROJECTION	**DETAIL/SPECIFICS**
Segmental Focus* On-premise Tactics	
Market Type Focus:	
Program Summary:	
Supplier Rep Plan:	
Promotions (detail type and frequency):	
Highlighted Accounts for Program Implementation:	
Ride With Plan:	
Crew Drives:	
Pub Crawls:	
Brew master Visits/Dinners:	
Sampling Programs:	
Other:	
Segmental Focus* Off-premise Tactics	
Market Type Focus:	
Program Summary:	
Highlighted Accounts for Program Implementation:	
Tactical Posts Planned:	
Ride With Plan:	
Crew Drives:	
Special Chain Programming:	
Sampling Programs:	
Other:	
Other Tactics	
Merchandising Themes/Programs per Quarter (if any):	
Qualifier request by Month(s) & detail:	
Incentive Program Frequency:	
New Package/Product Introductions:	
Sponsored Special Events/Activities Scheduled:	
Special Events to Guerilla (Not Sponsored):	

ANNUAL BRAND OVERVIEW

BRAND: _____

Brand KDA: _____

2016 Volume: _____

2016 vs. 2015 (up or down %): _____

2016 Case Volume Forecast: _____

% Up 2015 Forecast vs. 2016 Forecast: _____

LESSONS LEARNED in 2015

1- _____

2- _____

3- _____

4- _____

5- _____

2016 MARKETING/SALES STRATEGY: _____

Objective(s): _____

Tactics to Achieve 2016 Objective(s):

1- _____

2- _____

3- _____

4- _____

5- _____

Craft Brand "X" - Year-to-Date vs. CRAFT CLUSTER

Source:

Market Type	BRAND X 2019	BRAND X 2018	% Up or Down	% of Brand X Business	CRAFT CLUSTER 2019	CRAFT CLUSTER 2018	% Up or Down	% of CLUSTER Business
Convenience/Gas	1,807	1,840	-2%	2%	49,536	43,988	13%	6%
Drug Stores	916	937	-2%	1%	17,230	15,479	11%	2%
Liquor Stores	12,096	13,107	-8%	12%	102,891	97,590	5%	13%
Neighborhood Stores	18,327	19,412	-6%	18%	219,967	210,018	5%	27%
Spec Acc Off Prem	2	2	0%	0%	532	473	12%	0%
Supermarkets	22,514	23,328	-3%	22%	163,335	152,050	7%	20%
Wholesale Clubs	6,563	8,384	-22%	6%	37,472	45,572	-18%	5%
Adult Entertainment	296	416	-29%	0%	748	774	-3%	0%
Airlines/Lounge	5	2	150%	0%	335	303	11%	0%
Bar/Taverns	14,450	16,211	-11%	14%	59,466	60,169	-1%	7%
Bowling Center	202	267	-24%	0%	868	1,048	-17%	0%
Concessionaire	3,520	3,199	10%	3%	5,525	5,339	3%	1%
Golf Country Club	260	354	-27%	0%	2,295	1,861	23%	0%
Hotel/Motel	3,150	3,558	-11%	3%	4,868	4,914	-1%	1%
Music/Dance	2,699	3,541	-24%	3%	8,568	9,470	-10%	1%
Private Club	403	382	5%	0%	1,145	1,081	6%	0%
Restaurant	16,459	18,559	-11%	16%	138,196	130,640	6%	17%
Special Event	-53	1,037	-105%	0%	1,587	1,561	2%	0%
Sports Bars	917	1,306	-30%	1%	1,862	1,879	-1%	0%
Sub Job CO#2	4	21	-81%	0%	26	-10	-360%	0%
Misc House & Sub Dist	99	56	77%	0%	350	361	-3%	0%
TOTALS	**104,636**	**115,919**	**-9.7%**	**100%**	**816,802**	**784,560**	**4.1%**	**100%**
Chains	36,971	40,402	-8%	35%	274,824	267,683	3%	34%
"Majors"								
Safeway	10,352	11,308	-8%	10%	57,860	55,134	5%	7%
Bev-Mo	1,619	2,059	-21%	2%	12,052	12,144	-1%	1%
COSTCO	5,058	6,060	-17%	5%	27,129	32,613	-17%	3%
7-Eleven	1,580	1,663	-5%	2%	33,399	29,703	12%	4%
FoodsCo/Ralphs	5,040	4,182	21%	5%	33,727	30,301	11%	4%
Smart & Final	2,536	2,605	-3%	2%	34,664	28,272	23%	4%
Restaurant Depot	1,505	2,324	-35%	1%	10,343	12,959	-20%	1%
Lucky	1,041	1,289	-19%	1%	11,055	12,665	-13%	1%
On - Prem	42,305	48,347	-12%	40%	222,915	216,406	3%	27%
Off - Prem	62,333	67,513	-8%	60%	593,870	568,139	5%	73%
TOTAL	**104,638**	**115,860**	**-9.7%**		**816,785**	**784,545**	**4.1%**	

FOOTNOTES

1-*Beer Business Daily,* 1/23/14, p3
2- *Brewer's Association,* 2015 State of the Industry Address
3-*Brewer's Association* Podcast 5/2015
4-Gordon, Paul, Guiltinian, Joseph, P., *Cases in Marketing Management,* New York, McGraw Hill, 1991, pgs 147-157
5-ibid
6-*Beer Business Daily,* 4/14/15 p2
7-*Beer Marketer's Insights,* Verbal permission granted by Mr. Benj Steinman, owner to cite his firm's work
8- *Beer Marketer's Insights,* Verbal permission granted by Mr. Benj Steinman, owner to cite his firm's work
9-*Craft Business Daily,* 3/27/14 p1
10-*Brewer's Association* 2014 State of the Industry Address
11-Wikipedia
12- *eTalks,* on line interview with Dr. Philip Kotler and Niaz Uddin, 4/26/13
13-Craft Business Daily, 6/19/12 pgs 2-3, citing Scarborough Research and *Craft Business News,* 1/11/13 p3.
14-Kotler, Philip, *Marketing Management, Analysis, Planning and Control,* Englewood Cliffs, New Jersey, Prentice Hall 1980, pgs 289-302
15-Gordon, Paul, Guiltinian, Joseph, *Marketing Management Strategies and Programs,* New York, McGraw Hill, 1982, pgs 31-37
16-Aaker, David, *Strategic Market Management,* New York, John Wiley & Sons, 1984, pgs 6-8
17-*Beer Business Daily,* 4/8/14, p3
18-*Craft Business Daily,* 3/12/13, p3
19-*Guest Metrics LLC* News Blog, 4/5/13
20-*Guest Metrics LLC* News Blog, 1/28/13
21-*Guest Metrics LLC* News Blog, 3/25/13
22-*Beer Business Daily,* 3/23/14, p1
23-*Craft Business Daily,* 12/4/12, p2
24-*Craft Business Daily,* 5/23/14, p1
25-*Beer Business Daily,* 4/8/13, p2
26-*Beer Marketer's Insights,* 12/13/13 p2
27-*Beer Business Daily,* 11/6/33, p1
28-Keelson, Soloman, A., *The Evolution of the Marketing Concept: Theoretically Different Roads Leading to Practically Same Destinations!,* Online Journal of Social Sciences Research, Online Research Journals, April 2012, Vol 1, Issue 2, pgs 35-41
29-Wikipedia
30-Wikipedia

31-Colburn, Mark, W., *To Caffeine or Not to Caffeine, That is the Product Cannibalization Question*, 1984, University of Wyoming, Graduate School thesis.

32-McGuire, Edward P., Evaluating New Product Proposals, 1973, The Conference Board, pgs 92-93 & 98-105.

33-Kerrin, Robert A., Harvey, Michael G., Rothe, James T., *Cannibalism and New Product Development*, October 1978, Business Horizons, pgs 26-31

34-*Beer Business Daily*, 11/11/13, pgs 1-2

35-*Craft Business Daily*, 2/18/13, p3

36-*Craft Business Daily*, 1/11/13, p2

37-Hartley, Robert, F., *Marketing Successes Historical to Present Day, What We Can Learn*, New York, 1990, 2nd Ed, John Wiley & Sons, pgs 96-105

38-*Craft Business Daily*, 3/19/13, p4

39-Ibid

40-*Craft Business Daily*, 3/15/13, p2

41-*Craft Business News*, 5/3/13, p2

42-Miller, Tracy, *New York Daily* News On Line, 2/15/14

43-Wikipedia

44-*Craft Beer Daily*, 1/24/13, p3

45-Nielsen – State of the Media – The Social Media Report, 2012, On Line

46-*eTalks*, on line interview with Dr. Philip Kotler and Niaz Uddin, 4/26/13

47-*Beer Business Daily*, 4/13/13, p4

48-*Beer Business Daily*, Bump Williams quote, 8/26/14, pgs 1-2

49-*Craft Business Daily*, 3/15/13, p1

50-*Craft Business Daily*, 3/5/15, pgs 3-4

51-Brewer's Association, 2014 State of the Industry Address

52-*Beer Business Daily*, 3/2/14, p3

53-*Craft Business Daily*, 4/8/14, p3

54-*eTalks*, on line interview with Dr. Philip Kotler and Niaz Uddin, 4/26/13

55-*Craft Beer Daily*, 1/11/13, pgs 1-3